KNEELING
WITH
GIANTS

Learning to Pray with History's Best Teachers

GARY NEAL HANSEN

IVP Books

An imprint of InterVarsity Press
Downers Grove, Illinois

InterVarsity Press
P.O. Box 1400, Downers Grove, IL 60515-1426
ivpress.com
email@ivpress.com

InterVarsity Press® is the book-publishing division of InterVarsity Christian Fellowship/USA®, a movement of students and faculty active on campus at hundreds of universities, colleges and schools of nursing in the United States of America, and a member movement of the International Fellowship of Evangelical Students. For information about local and regional activities, visit intervarsity.org.

Scripture quotations, unless otherwise noted, are from the New Revised Standard Version of the Bible, copyright 1989 by the Division of Christian Education of the National Council of the Churches of Christ in the USA. Used by permission. All rights reserved.

While all stories in this book are true, some names and identifying information in this book have been changed to protect the privacy of the individuals involved.

Cover design: Cindy Kiple
Interior design: Beth McGill
Image: S. Greg Panosian/iStockphoto

ISBN 978-0-8308-3562-1

Printed in the United States of America ∞

InterVarsity Press is committed to ecological stewardship and to the conservation of natural resources in all our operations. This book was printed using sustainably sourced paper.

Library of Congress Cataloging-in-Publication Data

Hansen, Gary Neal, 1960-
Kneeling with giants: learning to pray with history's best teachers
/ Gary Neal Hansen.
    p. cm.
Includes bibliographical references (p.).
ISBN 978-0-8308-3562-1 (pbk.: alk. paper)
1. Prayer—Christianity. I. Title.
BV215.H346 2012
248.3'2—dc23

2012000262

P	20	19	18	17	16	15	14	13	12	11	10	9	8	7	6	5	4	
Y	32	31	30	29	28	27	26	25	24	23	22	21	20	19	18	17

For Dawna

CONTENTS

ACKNOWLEDGMENTS

I wish to acknowledge with gratitude the generous support of the Louisville Institute's Christian Faith and Life grant program.

I am also in the debt of my students and student assistants. Participants in my seminary prayer class have been a rich blessing to me and have kindly permitted me to share some of their comments and observations on the usually private experience of prayer. I particularly want to thank David Webster, Megan Smick, Christie John and Loren Shellabarger for help with bibliographic research and preparation of texts for the primary source reader.

Carol Spindel taught me crucial lessons about writing, and my fellow students in her seminar at the Iowa Summer Writing Festival provided genuine encouragement.

I also thank Mark Labberton, Greg Cootsona and Gary Jansen for their kind and generous help in the journey toward publication, and Cindy Bunch for her excellent editorial guidance.

If I only knew him, I would thank Leonard Cohen for providing the soundtrack to which most of this book was written.

I am above all grateful to my wife, Dawna Duff, for her constant kindness and support, for patience with reading multiple drafts and for excellent advice on each one, and for first suggesting I teach a class on prayer while writing the book to deepen my engagement with these great teachers and their ways of praying.

INTRODUCTION

This book will teach you to pray. In fact it will teach you ten different ways to pray, each one distinctly different from the others.

These are not all of the ways Christians pray, but each of these is authentically Christian, with deep roots in the practice of countless faithful disciples. We will explore each one with the guidance of someone who pioneered it, popularized it or famously practiced it, and who can serve as a helpful example. The approaches we study will span many centuries and include voices from Orthodox, Catholic, Anglican, Lutheran, Reformed, evangelical and charismatic traditions.

KNEELING WITH GIANTS

It is a pity that so many Christians do not have ways to pray that they find life-giving. Our infinitely creative God made each of us and wants us all to draw near, abiding in him as close as a branch is to the vine from which it grows. But countless faithful people learn one way to pray—from a book, their pastor or their own imagination—and if it does not seem joyful when they try it, they figure they are just not good at prayer.

Thankfully, that same infinitely creative God has prompted different people, in different traditions, places and times, to approach the task of prayer in a wide range of ways. I am convinced that there are enough deeply rooted, authentically Christian ways to pray for everyone to find one that fits. Maybe more than one.

This book will give you the chance to learn to pray from a variety of mentors. Most of them embody well-developed theologies of prayer, and even those whose theology seems problematic can open a door to begin exploring the spiritual life of a major Christian tradition. One or two may become your new companions in the way of Christ. If they teach you to pray in ways that help you grow closer to God, that is a very good gift.

The book will introduce theologically rich sources, but it is unabashedly practical. That solves two problems. First, some great books on prayer are *only* theological, answering every question except the crucial one: How do I do it? Some very influential voices tell us that we are able to grow as theologians only to the degree we are actually drawing close to God in prayer. Those we study will give us ways to start anew and ways to go further in the actual practice of prayer.

Second, quite a number of books introduce old or new ways to pray, but without taking seriously the range of Christian teaching on prayer through history. Some solid books teach one approach well—but that will not help every Christian. Others offer the wisdom of some great saint as your guide to prayer but only scratch the surface, and sometimes the saint in question did not actually teach anything about prayer. And some imagine creative new ways to pray, missing entirely the richness of practices that have nurtured the faith of millions.

FOR YOU, FOR OTHERS
Knowing a range of ways to pray that are undeniably Christian can be really valuable. It can help you personally if you are one of those who have found that prayer is basically flat and empty. I hope that as you read this book you will find one or two approaches to prayer that spark your imagination—ways of praying

that make something inside you say, "That fits. That is who God made me to be."

You may also find that certain approaches you dislike at first become very useful in some future season. If you take time to try on these ten ways of praying, the memory of them will stick with you. There are times when a change in our lives—from a tragic loss to a joyful new vocation—can make it simply impossible to pray as we used to. If you do not know any options, you are stuck, unable to pray even if you know prayer is crucial to survival. If you have even a little experience with other ways of praying, they are there for you when you need them.

The goal is not to practice all ten every day forever. The goal is to find a way to deepen your journey with God for the next season of your life. Just reading the book will not be sufficient, however. That would make it too easy to reject some of them without really understanding them. You will learn when you practice these ways of praying. If you spend two weeks on each one, praying that way for just fifteen minutes each day, you will get a much deeper sense of which ones appeal to you.

Your personal growth is not the full purpose. If your calling is to help others grow as Christians, I want you to be equipped to help them pray in ways that deepen their relationship with God. If their prayer is an authentic encounter with God, it will flow into serving Christ more passionately and effectively in the world.

To help people pray, you need to know about people, and you also need to know about prayer. Different people need to pray differently. Extroverts and introverts approach their human relationships differently, so it should not be surprising if their conversations with God are different too. Some people live in books and some in their senses; some need words and others need silence.

In terms of teaching about prayer, as the old saying goes, if the only tool you have is a hammer, pretty soon everything starts to look like a nail. If you learned the "ACTS" pattern (Adoration, Confession,

Thanksgiving, Supplication) you may find you teach it to a scientist or an artist, to the victim of an auto accident facing two months in a hospital bed or a father of four who just lost his wife to cancer. ACTS will not always help, even if it does have a catchy biblical acronym. Better to know some of the many approaches that faithful people have found useful for centuries. Only then can you help any particular person find ways to relate to God that really fit. Then, after really listening to the person before you, comes the joy of saying, "I think I know a way to pray that might really be helpful to you."

Prayer is incredibly important. St. Benedict, the founder of monasticism in the Western world, thought of prayer as "the work of God," a worthy lifetime occupation for countless thousands of monks and nuns. John Calvin taught that prayer was "the chief work of faith," the essential thing any Christian will do, no matter what else he or she is called to. Other theologians have other ways of emphasizing prayer's importance. The teachers in these chapters may differ in what prayer looks like, but they agree that nothing is more foundational for our life in Christ.

USING THIS BOOK

All readers, and especially those using this book in classroom settings, can read the electronic companion volume—the *Kneeling with Giants Reader,* which has a chapter of primary source readings to accompany each of the ten chapters—along with it. I urge you to make use of these readings as you go. Reading the great books that have taught these ways of praying to generations of Christians can be both enriching and baffling at times, but it can start you on a joyful exploration of the great spiritual and theological traditions that make up the church across the ages.

You can work through the book on your own of course, but it is also structured to make it easy for groups or classes to use. For those who want to lead classes and groups in studying this book, appendix two can guide you.

I have arranged the ten approaches into four groups. Part one has three ways of praying that guide us into the experience of using written prayers; these are words that have stood the test of time, all of them rooted in biblical prayers. If you find yourself unsure of what you might say to God, these three get you going in a healthy direction. Part two has two approaches to using the Bible in prayer. These are not the only ways to pray with Scripture, but they are solid examples, one focusing on how the Bible helps us speak to God, and the other on how it helps us hear God. Part three gives three examples that are more about our personal conversation or communion with God. There is something here for everyone: those who favor the spoken word, the written word or no words at all. The final section gives two views of what many people think of as the very definition of prayer: making specific requests for God to act.

However you go through this book, the one crucial thing is to pray. Even if what is described sounds totally unfamiliar, even if you cannot quite get how a particular approach is actually prayer, give it a try. In truth, a brief experiment is not enough to understand any of these approaches in depth; people have used them for a lifetime without exhausting them. That is how it should be. These are not techniques created on a whim, but gateways to whole spiritual traditions, ways to grow in a life-giving relationship with the God who created the universe and who redeemed us in Christ.

WHAT LANGUAGE
SHALL I BORROW?

He was praying in a certain place, and after he had finished, one of his disciples said to him, "Lord, teach us to pray, as John taught his disciples."

LUKE 11:1

Wh?hat can we say to the God of the universe? As St. Bernard of Clairvaux (1090-1153) put it in his Passion hymn, "What language shall I borrow, to thank you, dearest friend?" Lots of people find prayer baffling—even those we assume are experts. In a sense, we are all beginners, groping our way toward God on each new day.

All three ways of praying in part one of this book help us pray by putting words in our mouths, giving us language when we have none or giving us better words than we could think of ourselves. They all start with ancient prayers rooted in Scripture. Still, these three approaches could hardly be more different from each other. St. Benedict of Nursia taught his monks to pray using the words of the liturgies from the church's daily services. Martin Luther taught the early Protestants to use their own words, but to follow the outline of topics in the Lord's Prayer. And teachers in Eastern Orthodoxy have taught that we should pray by constantly repeating what they call the Jesus Prayer.

It is unlikely that any one person will be drawn to all three approaches, but that's fine. The point is for each person to find ways that fit his or her personality and needs, and to understand other ways that help other Christians to pray. Each one is the tip of an iceberg: below the surface of each is a great tradition of spiritual theology, a deep and rich way of experiencing the Christian life.

PRAYING WITH ST. BENEDICT

The Divine Office

On hearing the signal for an hour of the divine office, the monk will immediately set aside what he has in hand and go with utmost speed. . . . Indeed, nothing is to be preferred to the Work of God.

Brothers who work so far away that they cannot return to the oratory at the proper time . . . are to perform the Work of God where they are, and kneel out of reverence for God.

THE RULE OF ST. BENEDICT

When I was pastor of a struggling church, I took my annual study leave at a Benedictine monastery. Every few hours, a bell called me to the chapel. Standing between two monks, I said and sang the divine office, a cycle of eight daily prayer services, also known as the daily office. If "office" reminds you of the place where you earn your living, that is probably good: St. Benedict of Nursia (c. 480-c. 550), the father of Western monasticism, called this kind of prayer "the Work of God." It is also called the "liturgy of the hours." *Liturgy* comes from Greek roots meaning "the people's work" and refers to any scripted service of worship. In this view, prayer is how we labor in our calling as Christians, our core duty and key response to God. When we gather in God's presence, we join our voices to respond with prayer and praise and thanksgiving. It is the heartbeat of monastic life. You cannot overstate its importance. Benedict said, "Nothing is to be preferred to the Work of God," just as he said, "Let them prefer nothing whatever to Christ." Jesus is the highest priority, and prayer, day in and day out, brings us into his presence. For me, two blessed weeks of participating in Benedict's daily structure of prayer made room for rest, research and writing.

Without thinking about it, I had been praying in the tradition of Benedict all my life. In the Episcopal church I attended as a child, once a month we said Morning Prayer from the Book of Common Prayer. Instead of receiving the Eucharist, we recited psalms, heard readings and prayed responses. Later, as a university student, I went with hundreds of others, late on Sunday nights, into the Episcopal cathedral for Compline, the office for the close of day: with lights low, a choir sang ancient words of quiet trust in God.

Then, as a graduate student preparing for comprehensive exams, each day at dusk I trekked from the library to an Episcopal church where a handful of us took turns leading Evening Prayer. Still later I prayed the office alone using an old breviary, the Roman Catholic prayer book containing all the hours. I would roll out of bed in the morning, make coffee, sit in a comfortable chair and pray Prime, the first hour of the daily cycle, or Lauds, the service of praise that follows. Always the liturgy has led me to confession as well as praise, to praying for others as well as myself. Always it has used Scripture to give voice to my prayers as well as to help me listen to God.

Benedict's way of prayer is the "office," even when you pray it at home. Each service is an "hour," even if it takes only a few minutes. Essentially, it means praying the liturgies of services assigned for various times of day. It stretches me to pray in a healthy range of ways. It renews my connection to deep and holy things. When times are hard, it can put my battered soul back together. I admit there are also days when it feels like a ritual performed without conscious thought—though even that can help me. Whatever it feels like, it puts my day in a rhythm of prayer. As one of my students put it, Benedict envisioned a life of prayer with work interspersed, not the other way around.

Benedict specified seven services, or hours, in the daytime (since Psalm 119:164 refers to praising seven times a day) and a long "vigil" in the middle of the night (because Psalm 119:62 refers also to rising for praise at midnight). He matched each hour to the typical needs we face at that time of day: the vigil, called Matins, keeps watch for Christ while singing psalms and listening to Scripture; in the morning, Prime dedicates the workday ahead to God, and Lauds is filled with praise; Terce, Sext and None (at the "third," "sixth" and "ninth" hours of the day) briefly touch base with God, framing periods of work with prayer; Vespers, or evening prayer, brings work to a close; Compline helps us let go of the day and rest in God. Christians have prayed this way for most of two millennia, and they do so today—whether in the 1,500 or so monasteries and convents in the Benedictine tradition or in their own living rooms.

> *We believe that the divine presence is everywhere and that in every place the eyes of the Lord are watching the good and the wicked. But beyond the least doubt we should believe this to be especially true when we celebrate the divine office.*
>
> THE RULE OF ST. BENEDICT

When Thomas Cranmer (1489-1556) compiled the first Book of Common Prayer in 1549 for the Church of England, he simplified it for ordinary Christians by distilling the whole office into Morning and Evening Prayer—though current versions also include a short midday office and Compline. Either of these two main hours carries us through a wide-ranging conversation with God: We approach God speaking a sentence of Scripture appropriate to the season. God's light reveals our shadows, so next comes confession. God is merciful, so we hear the good news of forgiveness in Christ. Clean and fresh, we are ready to pour out our hearts in praise and lament, guided by the psalms. This leaves us ready to listen, and God speaks through Scripture readings. The Word prompts faith, so we affirm the Apostles' Creed. With the confidence of faith, we call out to God for our own needs and for the world. We give thanks. We receive God's blessing. By the end, our souls are well exercised; we have talked with God about more things in more ways than we probably would have remembered to on our own.

WHY BENEDICT?

"But," you say, "I am not a monk or a nun. I have a life to live. How am I supposed to stop and pray this way every couple of hours? And why would I want to pray from a book?" If you have spent years praying extemporaneously, the divine office may not seem like prayer at all. As one person bluntly told me, "It simply seems weird to pray other people's prayers during my personal prayer time." There is an irony in this of course: with every hymn or praise song, we pray other people's prayers without a problem. But those who are averse to ritual would agree with another who told me it can be difficult "to keep repeating the same old prayers over and over again." To them, liturgy was unfamiliar even in worship; they felt they were reading *instead* of praying.

Others, though, are quickly surprised at how helpful it can be. The liturgy frees them, keeps them on track, keeps them focused on their conversation with God. Praying the office has many benefits, but I will highlight four, for those who doubt.

First, praying the office can bring order to our busy lives. Even outside a monastery, people really can stop what they are doing and pray multiple times throughout the day. A billion and a half Muslims do it regularly: it is a pillar of Islam to pray five times a day, each time of prayer taking five to ten minutes. In a fifteen-minute break, a Western Christian can pray Terce, Sext or None and still have time for coffee.

Sheer busyness can keep us from regular prayer, as demands sweep us along like a river. Some say we become "human doings" instead of "human beings." Life feels at least slightly out of control, and we lose track of why we are doing what we are doing. Rather than a reason to avoid Benedictine prayer, this is a good reason to try it. Keeping an appointment with God even once a day is grounding; we refocus on who we are in relation to God.

With the office as a fixed part of my schedule, I find that even if the river sweeps me away, I know that I will soon hold onto a solid rock, breathe and find my bearings. This helps me especially in seasons that do not provide their own structure. For example, in graduate school I found that I got more done when I prayed the office and allowed that to structure my day. But it also helps away from work: on vacation I can better relax and enjoy freedom from work if I connect to God by praying a couple of the hours.

With the divine office, prayer begins to give the day its structure. If you pray morning and noontime prayer, the workday looks like two open stretches between times of prayer, rather than a frantic scramble punctuated by a sandwich crammed in at your computer terminal. The rhythm connects us to the eternal, so temporal demands fall into context. This is not squeezing prayer into a busy schedule. Prayer creates the schedule, so the day feels less busy and more productive. When we reconnect with God in a regular way, we have more of ourselves available to face the demands.

A second benefit of praying the office is that it teaches us how to pray. Some who are new to prayer tell me they have no idea what to say to God. Aren't we too small and insignificant to speak to the God who made heaven and earth? How can we speak to a holy God when we know our own weaknesses and failures so well? These are excellent questions, and in praying the office we find excellent answers. Spending a month praying just one of the hours can teach us what to say and how to say it. The office leads us through the whole range of ways people really need to pray: confession of sins, praise and thanks, asking for help for ourselves and others. It does these things with clarity, depth and wisdom. By giving us good words, the liturgy builds our skills. Then, when we go to pray on our own, what we have learned is waiting there to help us.

Even if we do not hold back before the Almighty, the office can be a valuable teacher. People who avoid formal ritual can still fall into ruts, with our prayers ringing the same notes every time. Our prayer lives are limited by our habits and our weaknesses. We may brood on our own needs or wallow in confession of our sins, but God is also worthy of praise and thanks. We may focus entirely on praise, even though the world suffers injustice and God's people in Scripture cry out in lament. For many, only intercession counts as prayer, to the exclusion of all the rest.

We need something to stretch us beyond ourselves. The office does just that. It pushes us toward a complete conversation with God. It prods the neurotically guilty to thankfulness, the obsessively grumpy to praise and the annoyingly cheerful to some honest complaint. It might even help us grow as people.

A third great benefit of Benedict's way of prayer is that it makes prayer possible in the hardest times of life. It often happens that a faithful Christian faces a tragedy only to find that he or she can no longer pray. Grief can undercut our sense of reality; God seems far away and familiar ways of living the faith become unreliable. It can leave us stunned into silence, like Job on the ash heap after everything in his life was destroyed. Or such a loss can make us so angry that we are not on speaking terms with God for a while. If we try to pray, our own words feel false, empty or painful. Paradoxically, we may know that prayer is the one thing that would help. With the divine office, all we have to do is read the words, moving through the liturgy. At first it may seem more like listening in on other people's prayers, but eventually we notice that some fragment of the service expresses our own longings—some biblical cry for help or bitter lament. Even convinced we can't pray, we find we actually have prayed.

Other kinds of pressures also make prayer difficult. One seminary student told of the competing demands of studies, ministry and relationships. All his energy went into communicating: teaching, preaching, writing papers, talking. He was fragmented and drained, but the liturgy brought relief. Praying in more of his own words felt like work, but the office made prayer possible: "I was able to delve into the words and thoughts of others, and appropriate them as my own. This structure ironically provided me with the freedom to just simply be in the presence of God." The words of the church at prayer carried him to God's presence like the friends who brought the paralyzed man to Jesus on a stretcher.

This student's words hint at a fourth common benefit of this kind of prayer: it can bring a sense of peace. There is no promise of particular feelings; if feelings are your goal, you are likely to be disappointed. But Benedictine prayer does things that make for peace. It provides a rhythm for living that returns us again and again to where we belong: in the presence of the God who loves us. Even after a brief experiment with the office, people tell me that it has a way of centering them, making them ready for other kinds of prayer or for the rest of their responsibilities. This is especially true of those who pray Compline. Quite a number actually report sleeping better after leaving the day in God's hands when they pray this gentle service.

In addition to the psychological benefit of sitting quietly and chilling out, peace comes from being in the presence of God, opening up possibilities for new kinds of prayer. One person referred to the office as a kind of refuge where she could enjoy God's glory and majesty, a brief respite from demands that allowed her to relish being in God's presence.

Benedict's way of praying has something to teach us; after all, if it were just empty, boring repetition, the monks and nuns of thousands of monasteries would not have kept at it for fifteen centuries. And it is something many Christians hunger for. Take as testimony the popularity of books like Henri Nouwen's *Genessee Diary* and Kathleen Norris's *Dakota* and *Cloister Walk*. If we explore Benedict's way of prayer, perhaps we can share in the spiritual vitality these books tell of. I think it helps to look more closely at each step of the process.

GETTING STARTED

The basic practice is simple: You decide what time of day you want to pray. You quiet yourself for prayer. You turn to the appropriate page of your prayer book. Then you read through the liturgy, speaking its words to God, letting it guide the order and content of your prayer.

Waiting to see which of the hours will fit into your day does not work. Like a trip to the gym, this type of prayer does not happen by accident. The hour has to go into the appointment book when the pages are blank, so that the rest of the day gets built around it. Eventually, prayer becomes a habit—a crucial one, like eating and sleeping, that keeps life working.

FINDING THE OFFICE

There are many versions of the divine office available, from the most traditional to the very new. I recommend Protestants start with a modern-language version of the Book of Common Prayer.

(You can find the daily office of the Church of England online at www.churchofengland.org/prayer-worship/join-us-in-daily-prayer .aspx. The American version can be found at www.missionstclare .com.) It is straightforward to start with either Morning or Evening Prayer, especially if you do not happen to live in a monastery, and either of these two hours provides a fuller, more well-rounded time of prayer than any single Benedictine hour. You can add the other main hour, Noontime prayer or Compline when it seems comfortable and desirable. In fact, you can do any combination of hours that works. Versions are available from Anglican churches in every part of the world. Other Protestant denominations have also developed offices for daily prayer, but Anglican versions build on Cranmer's beautiful, prayable language and solid theological content.

Catholics, and those who want to explore the Catholic office, have a number of options available, including the current official version, *Christian Prayer: The Liturgy of the Hours.* (You can find it online at www.universalis.com.) Those wanting a more truly monastic form of prayer can now get a lovely abbreviated version of a current Benedictine office in *Benedictine Daily Prayer: A Short Breviary.* The Second Vatican Council in the 1960s eliminated the hour of Prime and allowed more local variation in the office, so those wanting to find something closer to Benedict's original need to hunt up used books. Possibilities include translations of the *Monastic Diurnal,* or "day hours" of monastic prayer, which include everything except the vigil of Matins. The full office is found in pre-Vatican II breviaries, though these vary slightly from Benedictine practice.

If you dislike denominational liturgies, there are also versions by individuals, like Phyllis Tickle's four-volume *Divine Hours* or those produced in the life of particular fellowships, like the Northumbria Community's *Celtic Daily Prayer.* Any of them let you taste and see. I usually spend a year with a particular version of the office and then, at the beginning of Advent, start a new one. Keeping with a version for a while means I learn to pray it, but the occasional change helps me hear the words in fresh ways. Each version has pros and cons, so if the one you start with really irks you, try another. The point is not to find the perfect office, but to learn to pray. Pick one for a time, and begin.

FINDING YOUR WAY

Once you have a version of the office, start small. Pick just one of the hours, even if you want to pray the whole thing eventually. I recommend you choose the hour that fits your own best time for prayer. If in doubt, though, try Compline. This quiet little service at the end of the day has few daily variations, making it easy to learn.

The outline of each hour is simple, but it can take some time to find your way around. Here are the hard bits: In the Breviary, some things are written out fully only the very first time they occur; if you jump in at a later part of the book, they are mysteriously abbreviated. Several schedules are intertwined, including the cycle of daily hours for the day, variations for day of the week and changes for the seasons and celebrations of the church year. In the Book of Common Prayer, you often must flip to other parts of the book to include psalms or the prayers, known as collects, that gather together the church's concerns. Hearing the Scripture readings requires a Bible. Fear not: you do not need to do it all at once. It will grow on you step-by-step, and you really do not need to include every detail to pray with integrity.

Let's assume you are using the Book of Common Prayer and aiming to pray Morning or Evening Prayer. The first step is to open to the start and pray what you find in that section, start to finish. That is, ignore the instructions to go find missing parts. If you do that for a week or two, the office will begin to feel familiar, and you can begin to pray the words comfortably.

By that time, you will notice that you are missing out on the psalms, Scripture readings and collects. The easiest thing to add next is the psalms. Praying the psalms is the heart of the office— Benedict planned for his monks to pray all 150 psalms every week. (That sounds like a lot, but he was lightening up from the Desert Fathers and Mothers, who prayed them all every day.) The Book of Common Prayer makes it even easier, with a table assigning a psalm or two for each morning and evening of the year. Still easier, the American edition includes the entire Psalter divided into sixty portions—a monthly cycle of mornings and evenings. That would lead you to pray every psalm twelve times a year, stretching and broadening your conversation with God.

It is also easy to add the collects. You will already be familiar with some that are found within the daily liturgy, but there is a separate section of collects for each week of the church year, and another of prayers for various occasions. As you explore them, they prompt you to pray wisely and broadly. Some find that the memory of these prayers begins to shape the way they pray outside the hours.

There are also places in Morning and Evening Prayer for readings from the Old and New Testaments. Most of the service has been about forming the words we speak in prayer. A good conversation has two parts, though, and

We must always remember, therefore, what the Prophet says: Serve the Lord with fear, *and again,* Sing praise wisely; *and,* In the presence of the angels I will sing to you. *Let us consider, then, how we ought to behave in the presence of God and his angels, and let us stand to sing the psalms in such a way that our minds are in harmony with our voices.*

THE RULE OF ST. BENEDICT

so the office has us listen to God speaking through Scripture. There is a lectionary, or table of assigned passages for the whole year, or you can follow your own plan. I prefer to read books of Scripture from start to finish, so I pick one from each Testament and read a chapter a day at the assigned places. This means I keep my place in Scripture even if I miss a day of the office.

It is a little more complicated with a diurnal or breviary. Again, move from the simple toward the complex. Different editions have slightly different sections. In some, you should start with the Ordinary, meaning the basic form or outline of each hour without readings or seasonal variations. In others, you will find the starting place is called the Psalter, which will mean that the psalms are there in the ordinary outline for the whole week. When praying that is comfortable, you can explore sections where special prayers or readings are assigned to seasons and saints' days—these are labeled Propers if they refer to one specific celebration and Commons if they are applicable to a whole category of days.

Praying every specified part of the office requires patience— and some skill in flipping around to different sections. It may or may not grow on you. Do not despair. Simply praying the ordinary form of an hour with psalms comes pretty quickly and can provide a rich time of prayer.

Whether it feels exciting or a bit stiff, press on. Each hour is different, so try to get to know its "personality" before moving on to another. If it begins to feel boring, press on; you may move from familiarity to affection. Press on even if some parts bother you: Protestants may be troubled by the theology of some Catholic prayers, and many today cringe at traditional masculine language. Think of it as praying with your older, slightly curmudgeonly friends. Stick with it until you can enter the flow of the service. A solid try takes at least a couple of weeks; give it that before you switch to a different version.

You may come to look forward to certain responses, psalms or prayers, realizing they express the cries of your own heart. As one former Southern Baptist told me, "I can't put into words the peace I feel when I get to the phrases 'Lord, have mercy. Christ, have mercy. Lord, have mercy.'" Or perhaps you will be a complete convert, like the woman from a traditional Presbyterian background who exclaimed, "I love Compline! Love, love, LOVE, *LOVE* Compline!"

PROBLEMS AND POSSIBILITIES

However, first impressions are not always so positive, and the problems are not limited to being put off by written prayers. In a church adult-education class, I said we would close for the evening by praying Compline together. At that, one man who had seemed really engaged stood up and walked straight out the door. I asked the class to pray Compline for the next week as "homework" as well, so when we next met I asked how this had gone. The man who had fled spoke up. He left in protest, he said, because this was a Catholic form of prayer; nothing good could come from monasticism. For him, and for anyone with a similar background, perhaps this way of prayer is impossible, though I hope most can try to gather wisdom from traditions other than their own. Many Protestants find that this traditionally Catholic form of prayer helps them pray in ways that very quickly prove to be life giving.

There are other challenges: some find it odd to pray a liturgy alone when it has parts for multiple people, and some can't bear the repetition. If you just can't pray this way, that can be good discernment; move on to the next approach. The point of trying new approaches is not to keep praying in every possible way. The point is to find which ones fit you—and which ones don't. I hope you find the freedom in Christ to give the office a try for a few weeks, even if it means setting aside doubts, preconceptions and critiques for a time.

Experience teaches useful lessons, sometimes in surprising ways. I have heard people strongly object to the theology of certain passages of the office, only to find they were direct quotations of Scripture. When they get past initial difficulties with liturgy, many comment that one of the best things about praying the office is the company: the parts for other people to pray remind them that this really is prayer with the whole church.

A woman I know led Morning Prayer in an Episcopal church. A staff member asked one day who had come, and she said she had prayed alone that day. He responded, "What about the saints and the angels?" Even apart from angels and the faithful through the ages, when I have a bout of insomnia, praying Matins from my breviary reminds me that many others keep vigil with me. Whenever we pray the hours, we pray with countless Christians. We are surrounded by a great cloud of witnesses—thousands of monks and nuns as well as ordinary Christians across the boundaries of nations and denominations.

Even praying the office for a week or two can awaken us to new possibilities. If we are usually distracted, the words of the office keep our minds in prayer as the banks hold a river. People from traditions that are either rationalistic or enthusiastic are struck by the beauty and reverence of the office; with a fresh breeze of the Spirit, boredom with prayer gives way to awe. Occasionally, but regularly enough to mention, people tell me praying the office brings the opportunity for healing. Somehow it provides room to feel old griefs—a safe space to bring things to God with tears of sorrow or joy.

Perhaps some of these benefits come because the office forces us to pray. It is easy to miss the mark by reading books *about* prayer or books of devotionals; we can convince ourselves that we are passionate about prayer without actually doing it. Reading the office is different. The words of the liturgy *are* prayer, so we almost can't help speaking to God when we read them day after day. Of course, no one experiences every benefit, and some find no good at all in the office, even after giving it the good old college try. You can still keep the experience in mind for a different season of life or for someone else who might find it helpful.

As you consider trying the office, keep in mind two greater benefits, which may not be universal. The first is perspective: praying the office can help us see ourselves and all things in their proper relation to God. You see this in Benedict's own life, in the biography written by St. Gregory the Great (c. 540-604). Benedict began his monastic experience as a hermit in a cave, and there his life was formed by prayer. He emerged to serve as head of a monastery. His monks tried to poison him—which I suppose should be an in inspiration to all who have found ministry a struggle. He handled failure by returning to prayer, taking a season "to live alone with himself in the presence of his heavenly Father."

Gregory stops to explain what this meant for Benedict: "By searching continually into his own soul he always beheld himself in the presence of his Creator. And this kept his mind from straying off to the world outside." This was not a permanent retreat from conflict; Benedict returned to active ministry, and with great success. Prayer enabled him to see his life in perspective, in relation to God, and that equipped him to serve. His *Rule* shaped monastic life so that others could live the same life of prayer, the divine office framing a life of loving service in proper relation to God and neighbor.

For Benedict, prayer actually led to perspective on things much bigger than his own life. For a lifetime, he prayed in the stable rhythm of office, and between the hours we find him at prayer as well. At his window before Matins, Benedict saw a brilliant light from heaven and "the whole world was gathered up before his eyes in what appeared to be a single ray of light," Gregory wrote.

The light of holy contemplation enlarges and expands the mind in God until it stands above the world. In fact, the soul that sees Him rises even above itself, and as it is drawn upward in His light all its inner powers unfold. Then, when it looks down from above, it sees how small everything is that was beyond its grasp before.

The "work of God" had brought him to God's presence, where he could look at all of life in clear perspective. There is no promise of such visions, but the more of the hours you pray and the longer you keep at it, the better chance you have of keeping all of life in perspective.

Benedict intended prayer, including the office, to be a big part of life. In his thinking, monastic life was "a school for the Lord's service," and prayer was part of every lesson. Prayer was as constant and necessary as breathing, since the *Rule* called Monks to pray at every turn, even outside the hours, whether in private devotions or before starting work together in the kitchen. The office provided a prayerful framework, creating space for listening to God in between.

Outside a monastery, too, prayer should fill our lives. With the office we are given a structure to prompt prayer, rather than depending on our own initiative. Prayer draws us back, morning, noon and night, day after day. Prayer begins to give meaning to whatever we do in between the hours because prayer gives our days their structure. Nothing brings a deeper sense that in God we live and move and have our being.

Praying the office brings a second, less romantic benefit. When it comes to prayer, the office is like practicing the scales when you are learning a musical instrument. You may pick up the guitar hoping to play like Jimi Hendrix, or you may start the piano hoping to master Beethoven's "Emperor" concerto. Whatever your goal, when you meet with your teacher, you probably find you have to play scales. The exercises seem like the farthest thing from beautiful music, but keeping at it day after day, you learn the intervals and patterns that music is made from. Do them well and you can do what you want to do most.

The office is like that. Think of it as praying your scales. If you are going to pray well, you need to learn to confess, to praise, to give thanks, to lament, to make requests and many other things. The office takes you through each of them, teaching your heart and mind excellent ways of doing them. It builds the spiritual equivalent of muscle memory, so the skills of praying are there waiting for you when you need them. So even if you prefer other ways of prayer, you may want to keep praying the office. The best musicians still practice scales when they are warming up. Praying the divine office is not the only way I want to pray, but it is excellent exercise.

Throughout this book, other ways of praying will echo parts of the divine office. Something the office does in passing will be the main event for another teacher, so praying the hours can serve as preparation for all the rest. If you do not like the musical metaphor, think of yourself as an athlete doing stretches and lifting weights to be ready for a game, even though the actual sport looks very different from stretching and lifting. The office gets your prayer muscles in shape for these more intensive experiences.

As with an instrument or a sport, some parts of a new way of praying are easy, but going deep takes time. An experiment of a few days or weeks will give you a taste of the office, but it will be barely enough to know whether you might benefit from it in the long run. Mastery requires effort, and it is worth remembering that the many great spiritual teachers of the monastic tradition spent decades at this kind of prayer.

Of course, you may discover that this way of prayer absolutely fits the person God made you to be. You can find out if you join for a time in the chorus of voices around the world and across the ages, all doing the "work of God." Find a prayer book. Pick a time of day. Look up the relevant service. Start to pray.

2

PRAYING WITH
MARTIN LUTHER

The Lord's Prayer

For whenever a good Christian prays, "Dear Father, your will be done," God replies from above, "Yes, dear child, it shall be done indeed, in spite of the devil and all the world."

MARTIN LUTHER,
The Large Catechism

And should we so flippantly despise such might, benefits, power, and fruit—especially we who want to be pastors and preachers? If so, we deserve not only to be given no food to eat, but also to have the dogs set upon us and to be pelted with horse manure.

MARTIN LUTHER,
preface to The Large Catechism

Martin Luther (1483-1564), the leader of the Protestant Reformation, was a pastor. In his Large Catechism of 1529, he tried to nurture his people's relationship with God by teaching them how to pray—specifically how to use the Lord's Prayer. As well as helping us know what to say, Luther helps us imagine God's response: "Yes, dear child, it shall be done indeed, in spite of the devil and all the world." He is convinced that God is a good and loving parent—eager to listen, compassionate, generous.

In a preface to the same catechism, in words directed to other pastors, he is feistier. Here, too, he is discussing prayer and how we must not neglect it—including, and especially, the Lord's Prayer. If we do not make good use of this teaching, "we deserve not only to be given no food to eat, but also to have the dogs set upon us and to be pelted with horse manure." As well as revealing a bit of his character, in saying this Luther shows that he was, in fact, a bit of a character. He definitely shows why he is always fun to read. He was absolutely passionate about prayer, even if he did not match anyone's stereotype of a teacher of prayer.

Those two characterizations do fit into one person. He is passionate because he is a pastor. He is a shepherd tending God's flock, always tender toward the sheep, but easily angry with anyone who would threaten their well-being.

SCRIPTURE AND NEW LIFE

Luther's life changed when he began to study and teach the Bible at the new University of Wittenberg. When he started the job, he was a worried monk, striving with all his might to make himself acceptable to a God who sat in judgment. When he turned to Scripture, he discovered that God wanted nothing from him but faith. And when he trusted God to give him salvation in Jesus, he began to experience God as a loving father. Scripture drew him to new life, and he was convinced that the same would be true for any Christian.

When he went on an official investigation of the churches in his region, Luther was appalled at people's ignorance: "The ordinary person, especially in the villages, knows absolutely nothing about the Christian faith, and unfortunately many pastors are completely unskilled and incompetent teachers." He was probably not exaggerating much, since the education of priests was sorely lacking. If the priests knew little, the people had no way to learn.

Luther wanted to remedy the situation, so he started with the basics. He prepared catechisms to teach what every Christian needed to know: the Apostles' Creed, the Ten Commandments and the Lord's Prayer. A wise teacher, he started with these texts because everyone should have learned them already for their confirmation. Luther helped people explore them in depth as a summary of biblical faith, biblical ethics and a biblical way to relate to God in prayer.

Actually, Luther had already been writing on these things, and especially the Lord's Prayer. He wrote extensively on the Lord's Prayer throughout his career, and at least five of his expositions are available in English translation. His go-to response to the question "How should I pray?" was "Use the Lord's Prayer." It makes sense: the disciples asked Jesus to teach them to pray and his response was the Lord's Prayer. To Luther, this is not just a suggestion. Jesus was giving the best possible guidance, the very best prayer: "If he, the good and faithful Teacher, had known a better one, he would surely have taught us that too." As well as an invitation to pray and a promise that we will be heard, it is a command to pray for particular things.

Those who read broadly on prayer may find Luther's approach familiar. I find that for many Christians, though, his teaching is completely unknown. Getting his approach across is difficult for two reasons. First, for some, the Lord's Prayer is so familiar and beloved that they assume they are following Luther's advice even before they know what it is. Second, some who have experienced only rote recitation of the Lord's Prayer, and who dislike rote recitation, reject Luther's teaching in advance.

Luther sees prayer as crucial to living and growing in the Christian faith, and he sees the Lord's Prayer as important, but he is teaching a very particular use of the Lord's Prayer. Throughout his career, he taught the same basic practice, whether teaching Lutheran clergy or writing a letter to his barber. I suspect that his advice struck his readers as a whole new take on something they had known their whole lives. People today may find it just as revolutionary to their prayer lives, unless perhaps they are among the world's seventy million Lutherans. Luther can be a guide for all who need a fresh start in prayer.

THE BASIC METHOD

It is easy to describe Luther's basic method, as well as to say what it is not. He did not think the Lord's Prayer was primarily for rote recitation in worship. Nor, for that matter, is it something simply to rattle off in private prayer. Luther used the Lord's Prayer as an outline to structure a time of prayer—a framework that shapes prayers offered in our own words, our own meditations and requests, our praise and confession. It is Christ's authoritative guide to the *topics* we should pray. We stop on a clause and spend time praying in our own words on that subject, and then we move to the next one. Rather than leaving us to a completely open, even wandering, talk with God, Luther offers us a map to make sure we go through all the territory we really should cover.

I often recommend writing the Lord's Prayer out on a card and holding onto it, even if people already know it cold. They can put their thumb on one line, pray about that topic and then move to the next line. This can help people who find it challenging to slow down after decades of careening through it in worship. It also helps people who come from nontraditional churches in which the Lord's Prayer is not emphasized.

You should also know that I do not want you to recite all these words in your prayer. That would make it nothing but idle chatter and prattle. . . . Rather do I want your heart to be stirred and guided concerning the thoughts which ought to be comprehended in the Lord's Prayer. These thoughts may be expressed, if your heart is rightly warmed and inclined toward prayer, in many different ways and with more words or fewer.

A SIMPLE WAY TO PRAY

Luther's choice can have enormous benefits. First, using the Lord's Prayer as our outline ensures that we pray for a wide range of things. Clearly Jesus did not want our prayers to be dominated by a single issue, whether praise or confession or intercession. This can help those of us who tend to bring up the same issues over and over. Second, it reminds us that prayer is a requirement: Jesus commanded us to pray. Since Jesus said, "Pray then in *this way*" (Matthew 6:9, italics added), we can't leave these topics behind. With Luther's method, any time of prayer, short or long, can follow the pattern Jesus gave us. And third, according to Luther, this helps us pray with confidence. If Jesus commands us to talk about these things, by implication God promises to listen to these things. That can especially help people who are afraid to pray.

EXPLORING THE LORD'S PRAYER

There are two challenges to meet when using a text we know so well in a new way: First, we need to become aware of what each petition means theologically; second, we need to figure out what to say when we try to pray it. In both cases, we need to think harder about the Lord's Prayer than most of us usually do, even if we already say it—well—religiously.

In some of his writings, Luther simply explained the meaning of each line of the Lord's Prayer. I will do that too, bringing in Luther's reflections along with my own. In other texts, Luther gave actual examples of what he himself said to God when prompted by each line of the prayer. We will listen in on the Reformer's prayers to let his example prompt us to our own prayers. That is what he said we should do: he tells his readers not to try to use his words, but rather to follow his lead by praying through the topics in their own words.

Luther points out that even the outline of the Lord's Prayer teaches something important: The first two words establish an intimate conversation with the God who has adopted us as beloved children. The first three petitions guide us into the appropriate attitude, putting God's concerns first—God's name, God's kingdom, God's will. Then, and only then, God invites us to bring our own concerns, whether for food, forgiveness, guidance or other help.

"Our Father in heaven." In the address, we call out to God: "Our Father in heaven." This pulls our attention in two directions. On the one side, calling God "Father" assumes an amazing intimacy with the Creator and Ruler of the universe, and that can prompt us to praise and thanks. We have this intimacy, not because God is in general the parent of all humanity. This is the gracious gift of Jesus: he knew he was God's *only* begotten son, but he tells us to pray *"our* Father." We who are far from God, guilty and broken, are now invited into Christ's own family; we are adopted by God. We can praise God for more than forgiveness—in Jesus we are lifted up to fellowship with the triune God.

Then this profound intimacy is balanced by its opposite: the God who has drawn us so close is outside us, "in heaven." God is always beyond our control, greater, wiser and more powerful than we are. Wonder flows as we remember the One who spread out the heavens, who guides all creation to his own glory and who mysteriously called us each of us into existence. As we call out to our

Father, remembering that God is in heaven may stun us to speech-lessness—a humble silence that is a kind of praise.

Luther had a very difficult relationship with his own father, but he seems to distinguish easily between his feelings toward old Hans Luther and God. He saw this part of the prayer as very good news: "Now of all names there is none that gains us more favor with God than that of 'Father.' This is indeed a friendly, sweet, intimate, and warm-hearted word." Still, he seems to know that it can be a struggle for some to pray this; he frames his own prayer of these words as a request for God's help to grow into this rela-tionship: "Now through your mercy implant in our hearts a com-forting trust in your fatherly love, and let us experience the sweet and pleasant savor of a childlike certainty that we may joyfully call you Father, knowing and loving you and calling on you in every trouble." He let the words "our Father in heaven" lead him to reflect on his own relationship with God, turning him to pray for new life and deeper knowledge of God.

Here, with Luther's example of his own praying, is where the trouble starts for some. Reading Luther's prayers, people can get bogged down because he used words they would never pray. One person said memorably, "The extra gibberish is distracting to me." She really had too many things of her own to pray for to use the Lord's Prayer at all, she said, let alone Luther's exposition of it. Actually, that is fine—Luther did not want her to pray his words. Better to let Jesus' words prompt our own prayers, trusting that if we understand his prayer, anything we really ought to be praying for will come up under his categories.

"Hallowed be your name." Having called out to the beloved and mysterious God, we make our first request: Jesus has us pray that God's name be "hallowed," or "made holy." In biblical terms, the name of God points directly to God's essence—and, of course, nothing could be more holy. When we reach this part of the out-line, we take time to ask that God be honored in us and every-

where. We may offer praise and thanks for things that do reflect the holiness of God—places where God is known and honored, where love and peace and justice prevail. Or we may think of things in our lives, our churches or the world that do not honor God, and ask for help. We ask God to make us fit followers of Jesus, people who can rightly bear his name.

When Luther prayed this, he asked for a variety of things. Sometimes it was for help to honor God in behavior: "Grant us your divine grace that we might guard against all that does not serve to the honor and Glory of your holy name." In later years, he made it explicitly a prayer for evangelism: "Convert those who are still to be converted that they with us and we with them may hallow and praise thy name, both with true and pure doctrine and with a good and holy life."

"Your kingdom come." In the second petition, we ask that God's kingdom may come, and we face the same paradox: God is surely King of all creation already. The problem is that we do not live like God's citizens. Reaching this point in the Lord's Prayer, then, we spend time asking for God to reign more visibly and thoroughly.

But what do we pray for when we pray for the kingdom? Scripture guides us to include a number of things. The kingdom is made up of those who call Christ their Lord, so we pray for more to come to faith and for those in the church to really live under his rule—for mission in terms of evangelism and discipleship. Our King fed the hungry, healed the sick and cared for the outcast, so we ask God to make these priorities ours too— for mission in terms of service and justice. The kingdom will be fulfilled only when Jesus returns, so we join the early Christians waiting eagerly, praying, "Maranatha! Come Lord Jesus!" As we turn to reflect on our lives, we ask God's ways to shine in our relationships, our work, our churches. We need to bring all of life before our Lord, asking him to reform it according to his sovereign intentions.

Luther starts with himself and the church, praying, "May we become your kingdom so that in heart, feeling, and thought we may serve you with all our strength inwardly and outwardly, obediently serving your purpose, being governed by you alone and never following self-love, the flesh, the world, or the devil." If we are not living as God intends, Luther thinks we are robbing God of territory where he should reign—our hearts—and living like citizens of the kingdom of the devil. He was also particularly aware of the opponents of the church and its work, and he prayed with tenderness and passion, "They are many and mighty; they plague and hinder the tiny flock of thy kingdom who are weak, despised and few. . . . Dear Lord, God and Father, convert them and defend us."

"Your will be done, on earth as it is in heaven." In the third petition, we pray that God will do what God wants done. By praying this we humble ourselves, openly acknowledging that God's plans are more important than our own. This petition is paradoxical, like the earlier ones, since surely God guides the world with or without us. Mysteriously, though, in God's design we are made partners in his planning, and it seems that God's will does not get done unless we pray. As well as prompting humble thanks, this should give us confidence that our prayers matter. As Luther said of the whole of the Lord's Prayer, "He himself commanded us to pray like this and promised to hear us." It is hard to imagine a higher honor.

Because of this partnership, this clause can lead us to confident intercession. In Jesus' teaching and his actions, we learn in detail what God's will looks like. Then when we pray for God to heal the sick or feed the hungry or bring justice and peace, we can say, "Thy will be done! I am confident that this is your will because you said so yourself. I'm just asking you to do what I know you want to do." This is no guarantee that God will do what we ask, but it does prompt us to pray in the spirit Jesus seems to intend. We pray for our lives, our churches and the world to look more like what God intends and for God to overcome every kind of opposition to his kingdom of love.

In another sense, this clause is about self-examination. Luther knew his own will always got in the way. "O Father," he prayed, "do not let me get to the point where my will is done. Break my will; resist it. No matter what happens, let my life be governed not by my will, but by yours." He suggested we look hard at the ways we willingly seek ungodly goals and at selfish motives we disguise as good. There is plenty of room for confession here if we find we have acted as if our will is more important than God's. This can also be the place to ask for help in the struggle to live as God calls.

We ask God to transform our will and to let his own good priorities work in the world, but there is more to it: we pray for God's will to be done in a particular way: "as it is in heaven." That is, with clarity and joy, with the efficiency of the angels—rather than with confusion, resentment and procrastination.

"Give us this day our daily bread." After three petitions about God, we turn to ourselves. This fourth clause starts with the very simplest human need: we need food to live, and bread is as basic as it gets. No concern is too small for God to care about or too great for God to manage. We take the time to ask for food, clothing, shelter, work, relationship. If we are well provided for, we can pray for those who are not. Jesus' point is that God wants to provide whatever we need, so whatever we need should be part of the conversation.

This petition gives us both a permission and a challenge. We are permitted to bring our mundane personal needs to God in prayer. Actually, it is more than an invitation: Jesus commands us to pray for our bread. He wants us to acknowledge that we are always dependent on God for everything. But we are also challenged to simplicity, not luxury; we are not praying for daily cake. Of course we can talk to God about anything, even our desire for luxuries. However, this petition gives us the confidence of a promise only when we ask for what we really need. Jesus gives us a measuring stick: we should pray for what is really good for us and for the world.

Early on, Luther focused this petition on the world's need for Jesus, since he is the bread of life: "Therefore, O heavenly Father, grant grace that the life, words, deeds, and suffering of Christ be preached made known and preserved for us and all the world." Later he came to see that by "bread" Jesus may have actually meant bread. That prompted him to pray for all the things that sustain earthly life:

> Grant [the emperor] wisdom and understanding to rule over his earthly kingdom in peace and prosperity. . . . Give us favorable weather and a good harvest. I commend to thee my house and property, wife and child. Grant that I may manage them well, supporting and educating them as a Christian should.

Both of these prayers are important. We do need Jesus, the true bread of heaven, and we need ordinary bread too. It sounds very dated to think of "managing" our families along with our property, but Luther has a point: God welcomes our prayers for every practical need, from food and clothing to peace and good government.

"And forgive us our debts, as we also have forgiven our debtors." From the practicality of bread we turn to intangible spiritual needs: in the fifth petition we ask forgiveness. We may be used to saying "trespasses," "debts" or "sins." Different churches use different translations of the Gospel passages, but the point is the same. We admit where we have done wrong, and we ask God to restore us. We take time to seek reconciliation to God and neighbor. It takes effort to look at our lives and courage to admit to actual faults, even in prayer.

Here we pay attention as well to the harm others have done us, and we talk to God about forgiving them, since we ask forgiveness "as we also have forgiven our debtors." Sometimes Luther treated this as an explicit condition: "We must first forgive our debtors. When we have done that, then we may pray 'forgive us our debts.'" In practice, though, he let these words prompt him to work at forgiving others, hand in hand with God:

> Grant forgiveness also to those who have harmed or wronged us, as we forgive them from our hearts. They inflict the greatest injury upon themselves by arousing thy anger in their actions toward us. We are not helped by their ruin; we would much rather that they be saved with us.

That is a useful model: by asking God to forgive others, we, too, take steps toward forgiving. That kind of prayer is better than forcing yourself to say you forgive when you do not or telling yourself that you can't forgive. Forgiveness is not pretending that no harm has been done—that is denial. Nor does it mean the painful feelings all melt away—that is healing, which may come much later. Forgiveness is when you have been harmed, but you actively, prayerfully lift the sentence and decide not to exercise your right to prosecute or avenge.

Praying other parts of the Lord's Prayer has probably already revealed some of our shortcomings. We fail to honor God's holy name or live under God's reign; we fail to do, or even know, God's will; we grasp for things well beyond daily bread. As we pray for the kingdom when God is already reigning, we paradoxically pray for forgiveness when God has already forgiven. Praying for forgiveness is about living into what is already true, recognizing and accepting the forgiveness Jesus offers. This puts us in a different relationship to God—humble and grateful. As Luther prayed,

> Dear Father, I come to you and pray that you will forgive me for this reason: not because I can make satisfaction or deserve anything by my works, but because you have promised and have set this seal on it, making it as certain as if I had received an absolution pronounced by you yourself.

In Jesus, we are already forgiven, but the Lord's Prayer keeps us honest: every time we pray we admit that we bring nothing to the relationship but debts—and every time we pray we take a little step toward receiving grace with confident trust.

"And do not bring us to the time of trial." The traditional translation of the sixth petition is "Lead us not into temptation." This may seem puzzling, since the letter of James says God never tempts us. But both Luther and modern translators of the Lord's Prayer point out that *temptation* can be translated *trial.* Either way, this petition is important. Thinking of temptations, we ask God to guide us, leading us away from anything that draws us from the way of Christ. Thinking of trials, we ask God to spare us mercifully. And if we are so blessed as to have no trials or temptation, it is an excellent opportunity to pray for others who do.

Luther treats temptation under the headings of the world, the flesh and the devil. All three concepts have fallen on hard times in our culture. But we still need ways to think about temptation that are specific but not simplistic, so Luther's categories are worth exploring.

We may hesitate to think of "the world" as a problem. God called creation good, and today it is easy to see human beings as sinning against the world. Luther meant something else: the negative influence of society on our character and behavior. Among other things, he prayed for protection against greed and lust for approval and power.

"The flesh" may make us think of ascetic extremists. We reject simple hatred of the body for good reasons. God came to us in human flesh, and those who reject their own bodies endanger their lives. Luther was no ascetic: he took pleasure in his relationship with his wife, Katharina, and in the beer she brewed for him. The temptation of the flesh is when we want to misuse its pleasures. Luther sounds modern when he complains, "The whole world is filled with stories and songs about wenching and harlotry, as though that were perfectly right." He sounds humble when he prays, "Help that we may withstand excesses in eating, drinking, sleeping too much, idleness, and laziness." Luther sounds wise praying about lust, asking that seeing someone attractive might be "an occasion for cherishing chastity and praising you in your creatures."

When Luther speaks of "the devil," the issue is spiritual temptation. He wants us to pray against anything that would cause us to disrespect God's Word, anything that is able "to tear us away from faith, hope, and love, to draw us into unbelief, false security, and stubbornness, or, on the contrary, to drive us into despair." If we do not know of these temptations, we simply are not paying attention. We desperately need God's help to avoid them.

But rescue us from the evil one." The seventh and last request is that God would "rescue us from the evil one," or as the more familiar translations put it, "deliver us from evil." Praying this means asking God for protection from all the things that worry us. If we feel comfortable, this petition reminds us that God is constantly preserving us from countless troubles that we do not even notice. And of course we should remember that the Lord's Prayer is corporate: "Deliver *us*" we pray, and so we take time to lift up the millions around the world who really are in danger.

Evil may seem too strong a word, but to Luther it means any kind of danger: he prays for protection against fire and flood, famine and war, even venereal disease; and after death, deliverance from judgment. When he reaches this last petition, he prays, "Protect us from every bodily evil and woe, to the end, however, that all this may rebound to the honor of your name, the increase of your kingdom, and [the accomplishment] of your holy will. Amen." In this you can see how he prays even the last clause in light of the first three petitions. He is convinced that all our prayers should be shaped by the priority on God's name, God's kingdom and God's will.

The familiar ending to the prayer, "For the kingdom, the power, and the glory are yours, now and forever," is not found in the earliest New Testament manuscripts or in the Latin Vulgate used in the Middle Ages. Luther does not comment on it. I do pray this conclusion. Saying, "For the kingdom, and the power, and the glory are yours, now and forever," I declare that the God I pray to is fully able to hear, strong enough to answer and wise enough to work out all the details. The fact that others may be praying exactly the opposite things is not a problem to God. And what I want is for God to answer in ways that bring his glory and his own kingdom. That means I come full circle, concluding with praise just as I began.

This in short is the way I use the Lord's Prayer when I pray it. To this day I suckle at the Lord's Prayer like a child, and as an old man eat and drink from it and never get my fill. It is the very best prayer, even better than the psalter, which is so very dear to me.

A SIMPLE WAY TO PRAY

GETTING STARTED, REAPING THE BENEFITS

You may be thinking that all of this is a bit overwhelming, with too many things to pray for. Can you actually pray for all these things every time you say the Lord's Prayer? Yes and no. If you try to do it all thoroughly, you may get bogged down and discouraged. I recommend starting with a very short time—perhaps five or ten minutes—and praying through the whole Lord's Prayer. Try to say just one or two sentences on each petition. Praying on every clause even briefly begins to train the heart in Jesus' priorities. It is a healthy reminder to pray in a well-rounded way, pushing beyond habitual and comfortable topics. Then, as you get familiar with the kinds of things that you want to say on each topic, you can expand the time.

Those who really dive in often find that they can't get through the Lord's Prayer in one sitting. That's good! Luther himself told his barber that he didn't need to go through it all at once: "I may get lost among so many ideas in one petition that I forego the other six." When that happens the thing to do, he says, is to listen to the Holy Spirit. Better to chew on one part that grabs your heart and mind. It works well to take one petition each day and pray through it thoroughly, going through the whole Lord's Prayer once in a week.

Maybe you are new to prayer and think Luther's approach sounds good. Like a shy person on a blind date, you may want a list of topics to bring up to help you during conversation. Or maybe your church teaches that intercession is the main event in prayer, and you wonder what to say once you have poured out your own current concerns. You may sense that following Jesus' list of topics will give you more to pray about. Still, you may wonder just how to work through each line of the prayer.

There are three practical tools that Luther uses, though he never lists them. First, it helps to think of what Jesus says to pray for in three time frames: each petition is in a sense accomplished already, and we give thanks; each petition applies to current needs, and so we ask; each petition will be truly fulfilled only at the end of the age, and so we wait with longing. Second, it helps to think about each clause of the prayer in concentric circles: we pray for God to answer in our own lives, then among our families and friends, then in our churches, our communities and the world as a whole. Though he prays for himself, Luther reminds us that the Lord's Prayer always says "our" and "us," rather than "my" and "me": "A prayer spoken only in behalf of oneself is not a good prayer." Then third, each line of the prayer can include more than one kind of prayer: within any line we may be led to quiet contemplation, words of praise and thanksgiving, and humble confession, as well as requests in the form of supplications for ourselves or intercession for others.

Luther taught this as a practice for a lifetime, not just an experiment, and it certainly shaped him as a Christian. As with any new approach to prayer, you would be wise to try it for a few weeks before trying to decide whether it is helpful to you. Some people have frustrating experiences the first week; it is surprising how often a second week is much more positive. If you are drawn to Luther's style of prayer, you will find more to work with in his writings. In similar ways, he prays through the Ten Commandments and the Apostles' Creed, and other texts as well. But the Lord's Prayer is the heart of his practice.

"AMEN!"

We left off one important word from the Lord's Prayer and Luther's exposition: "Amen!" For Luther this was not just a Christian equivalent to "So long for now!" It is the crucial conclusion that shows our faith in the God who hears our prayers. I will close with Luther's comments on the "Amen"—he always wanted to have the last word, anyway:

> Finally, mark this, that you must always speak the Amen firmly. Never doubt that God in his mercy will surely hear you and say "yes" to your prayers. Never think that you are kneeling or standing alone, rather think that the whole of Christendom, all devout Christians, are standing there beside you and you are standing among them in a common, united petition which God cannot disdain. Do not leave your prayer without having said or thought, "Very well, God has heard my prayer; this I know as a certainty and a truth." That is what amen means.

3

PRAYING WITH THE PILGRIM

The Jesus Prayer

> But the tax collector, standing far off, would not even look up to heaven,
> but was beating his breast and saying, "God, be merciful to me, a sinner!"
> I tell you, this man went down to his home justified.

LUKE 18:13-14

> The Gospel and the Jesus Prayer are one and the same thing. . . . For the
> divine name of Jesus Christ contains in itself all Gospel truths. The holy
> fathers say that the Jesus Prayer is an abridgment of the entire Gospel.

THE PILGRIM'S TALE

I gave my prayer class at the seminary a simple assignment: Say
the Jesus Prayer for five minutes a day. That is, just sit quietly and
repeat, "Lord Jesus Christ, Son of God, have mercy on me."

At the next class, a particularly bright student spoke up. He had
already earned an M.A. in English literature, taught courses, published poetry. "This has been, far and away, the most frustrating
prayer discipline for me."

I asked to hear more.

"I can't say that I completely get it. I've been able to see the value in each model we've studied so far, and I've benefited from them. But I can't say I've gotten much from the Jesus Prayer."

"Maybe it will be different after another week of practice." I live in hope.

"I don't know. I struggled with keeping my attention on the prayer for just five minutes."

Fast forward. At the end of the year, my students had a week with no assigned method, and I asked how they had prayed. My literary scholar spoke up: "My lease is ending, and I don't have a job. I have interviews in two states, final papers in four classes and my in-laws coming for graduation. All I can pray is 'Lord Jesus Christ, Son of God, have mercy on me' over and over!"

In this chapter, we will look at an approach to prayer that is a foundation stone of spiritual life in the Eastern Orthodox Church. It may seem utterly foreign, especially to Protestants—until, like my student, you hit a rough patch.

THE PILGRIM'S TALE

My exploration of the Jesus Prayer began in seminary when I came across an old, worn copy of a book called _The Way of a Pilgrim_, also known as _The Pilgrim's Tale_, in the library. I had heard of this book that brought Orthodox spirituality to the West. Tingling with curiosity, I read the story of a nineteenth-century Russian peasant. He traveled around on a spiritual quest: he wanted to learn how to do as the apostle Paul said and "pray without ceasing" (1 Thessalonians 5:17). How could he possibly pray every moment of every day?

Eventually he met an old monk, a _starets_, or elder, who told him he should pray the Jesus Prayer: "Lord Jesus Christ, Son of God, have mercy on me." He should repeat it over and over until it became "unceasing, self-activating prayer of the heart." The elder assigned a set number of times to repeat the prayer each day. Every time the pilgrim visited, the elder increased the number. Eventually he was saying these words twelve thousand times a day. His life became so steeped in the Jesus Prayer that he prayed it in his sleep; he woke to find his lips forming the words over and over. After that, he could no sooner stop praying than stop breathing. He truly was praying without ceasing.

The book is written in the pilgrim's own voice, and it reads like something between an impossibly miraculous memoir and an improbably pious novel. Scholars have shown that the work is not the actual history of a particular peasant. It evolved in the telling and retelling by a number of writers or editors, and portions of known works by an anonymous nineteenth-century Russian priest are woven into it. The events may be fictional, but the book tells of something true: the repetition of the Jesus Prayer really is an ancient and traditional approach to prayer. Plus, the book is a good read.

The Pilgrim's Tale is the simplest place to learn the practice at the heart of *hesychasm*, or stillness, a spiritual ideal of Orthodoxy. Prayer leads us to quiet, inward stillness in the presence of God, where we are neither distracted by passions nor pouring out noisy words. Why, if the goal is stillness, does one endlessly repeat the Jesus Prayer? Because it helps. Bishop Kallistos Ware, an influential scholar of Orthodoxy, puts it this way: "The mind needs some task which will keep it busy, and yet enable it to reach out beyond itself into stillness." The Jesus Prayer is a crucial tool, quieting mind and heart, focusing the attention on the gospel. It is, as we will see, about the gospel.

This tradition is taught in depth in the volumes of the *Philokalia*, a collection of spiritual writings dating from the fourth to the fifteenth centuries. The pilgrim's elder quotes the *Philokalia* to summarize the process:

Sit in silence and alone. Bend your head. Close your eyes. Breathe ever more quietly. With the imagination look inside your heart. Carry your intellect, that is your thought, out of your head and into your heart. As you breathe say quietly with your lips or in your intellect alone: "Lord Jesus Christ, Son of God, have mercy on me." . . . Try to drive away your thoughts. Keep restful patience and repeat this process very frequently.

The Jesus Prayer is a tool to bring the whole person together—heart, mind and body—into the presence of God. There, in holy awe, passions and thoughts are stilled. Ware quotes a Russian saint, Theophan the Recluse (1815-1894), as saying, "The principal thing is to stand before God with the intellect in the heart, and to go on standing before him unceasingly day and night until the end of life." The *hesychast*, and anyone who prays the Jesus Prayer, wants to draw near to God. It takes preparation, but of a paradoxical kind. God is not in a place you can get to with your body. God is not reached by your intellect alone, even if you study Scripture and theology. Feelings and emotions will not bring you to God. To approach God, one must bring all of one's self, with the intellect drawn into the heart, a unified whole.

It requires some effort at trans-

In no great length of time I felt that the prayer somehow was beginning to move into my heart by itself. That is it seemed that as it beat normally my heart began to form the words of the prayer inside itself with every heartbeat; for example, at the first beat, Lord; at the second, Jesus; at the third, Christ; and so on. I stopped saying the prayer vocally and began to listen carefully to my heart speaking.

THE PILGRIM'S TALE

formation to get to such a state—some effort of repentance, really, a change of mind and life. The Jesus Prayer is a tool to bring that change, to bring the mind into the heart and bring all before God in stillness. Then the praying Christian seeks to remain there, in the presence of God. It is thus a contemplative kind of prayer: drawing near to God, we use the Jesus Prayer to remain before God, breath by breath, aiming our gaze toward God. If we drift away, we use the Jesus Prayer to return, drawing near once again to God.

The *Tale* shows the pilgrim on this path, and the closer he gets to God, the more his life is filled with miracles. The point of these stories is to motivate the reader to try the Jesus Prayer and to show that the goal of unceasing prayer is a changed life. It did not bring worldly success. The pilgrim remained a peasant, begging for food or working odd jobs, but he began to find deep joy through prayer. And he began to look at the world through new eyes, seeing God at work in everything around him and everyone he met.

As people try praying this way today, they too tell of their perspective changing. One told me that as she prayed the Jesus Prayer, her mind wandered to her own problems, but those problems began to look different in light of the merciful work of Christ. If a way of praying can change my heart and make me more aware of God, I think it is worth giving a try.

THE PROCESS

It takes a while to learn and experience the benefits of the Jesus Prayer—or any new prayer approach, for that matter. The *Philokalia* assumes that we are Orthodox monks, and the writers would probably tell us to pray under the guidance of a knowledgeable spiritual director. It is good advice: the puzzling language of bringing the intellect into the heart hints at a very serious process. But if we want what the prayer actually asks for—the mercy of Christ— then it is more important to start praying. One should at least be grounded in a church community, living as a follower of Christ who worships, learns from Scripture and receives the sacraments. Better still, though, we should seek companions in the way of prayer, whether through spiritual direction or a prayer group.

I think learning to pray this way happens in three stages.

Stage one: Saying the prayer. The goal may be "unceasing, self-activating prayer of the heart," but the first step is in our bodies, in the act of saying the prayer—a lot. The task is just to say the prayer, pacing it with our breath, either silently in the mind or, better still, quietly with the mouth. If we form the habit of saying the Jesus Prayer, it becomes a little like a song that runs through the back of our minds, though not in an annoying way. For some, even at the beginning this focuses the mind on prayer and brings a sense of calm. Others find the exercise empty and frustrating. No particular feelings are promised.

 I know three good ways to approach this. First is what you see in *The Pilgrim's Tale.* Pick a number of times to say it each day, and once that becomes easy, increase the number. The elder gave the pilgrim prayer beads to keep count, but the traditional Orthodox tool is a prayer rope, or *chotki*, a ring of cord with thirty-three or more knots that can be held or worn around the wrist. Each time you say the Jesus Prayer, you move to the next knot. Eventually it becomes a physical and mental habit.

A second method many find easier is to pray the Jesus Prayer for a fixed amount of time, say five minutes per day. That can be worked into anyone's life: at daybreak or in bed before sleep, before getting out of the car after a commute or on a coffee break. Then, at a pace that feels comfortable, say the Jesus Prayer over and over. Some set a timer so they can focus without glancing at the clock, though it can be a bit jarring to be drawn from prayer with an alarm bell. When that is comfortable, expand the time. Eventually the prayer will find its way into other parts of the day.

Some I've worked with who found it quite difficult to do nothing but repeat the Jesus Prayer, even for a few minutes, developed a third method: they left notes here and there reminding them to pray. Then when they stood in front of the bathroom mirror, when they opened the fridge or when they sat down at their computer, they were prompted to say the Jesus Prayer. The more often we are reminded to spend a few moments praying the Jesus Prayer, the closer we are to praying it unceasingly. Similarly, some found it was much easier to practice if their bodies were busy, so they said the Jesus Prayer as they exercised or drove or made dinner.

It does help to pray along with your breath, as the elder taught the pilgrim. Breathing in, say "Lord Jesus Christ, Son of God." Breathing out, say, "Have mercy on me." The action and the words support each other: as we take in life-giving breath, we call on Jesus to hear and be present; as we exhale we ask for mercy, letting go of physical tension and giving God our burdens. Others prefer to pray it more slowly still, savoring one word with each breath. I find any physical rhythm helps, so sometimes I say each word along with a step while jogging.

There is also a more ancient way of practicing the Jesus Prayer, though Ware says that few use it today. One sits on a low stool and brings the head down toward the chest, which embodies the idea of moving the intellect to the heart. In this cramped position, the eyes are closed and the prayer is repeated along with the breath. Praying in a physically uncomfortable position does not appeal to me personally. Better, I would say, to choose an approach that seems as comfortable and natural as possible as you create the physical and mental habit of saying the prayer.

Stage two: Praying the meaning of the words. Between repeating the prayer and experiencing the transforming stillness of God's presence, there is more to do. Since, as the Orthodox say, the goal is unceasing prayer with the intellect in the heart, work next on the intellect. We need to move past repeating the prayer to meaning every word. Think about the words. Meditate on them. Then, praying along with your breath, focus on the meaning of the Jesus Prayer with all the energy and attention you can muster.

This is harder. Many find they can't pray concentrating on the meaning of the Jesus Prayer for very long at all, much less "without ceasing." However, it is crucial. We began with the body, but the content of the prayer guides the journey of the mind to the heart.

The prayer's form is simple: "Lord Jesus Christ, Son of God, have mercy on me." Ten words in English, six addressing the One who hears our prayers and four making our request. The words and phrases are familiar from Scripture. It is simple, but not simplistic. These ten words contain the kernel of all prayers, and they have the power to reorient your life toward Christ. This is elemental prayer, prayer distilled to its potent essence. Examined one by one, every word and phrase of the Jesus Prayer takes us to the very heart of the matter.

"Lord." Calling out "Lord," we place ourselves in proper relation to the One who hears our prayers. Though we also truly call him Savior, the basic shift of Christian living is from being our own boss to having a lord. My Lord is in charge, and I am his servant. I am accountable to my Lord: I must choose to please the One whom I serve rather than choosing primarily to please myself.

This should change the way we pray. We do not speak to someone who serves us, but to someone whom we serve. Prayer is a privilege. We should imagine ourselves entering the heavenly throne room, blessed to be granted an audience with our Ruler. We are in no position to make demands. We have no inherent right to get what we want when and how we want it. Praying "Lord" refocuses our attitude so we approach God in humility and awe.

"Jesus." The idea that we pray to a lord may trouble us. If we are subjects and he is King, will he "lord it over us"? Will God be demanding or capricious? Thankfully, the prayer continues and we find our Lord is "Jesus." Praying his holy name, we know the One to whom we pray.

This is good news. The Gospels show us who Jesus is. Our Lord is the one who welcomed the children and blessed them. Our Lord is the one who took rough-hewn fishermen, homemakers and tax collectors and made them his preachers, theologians and missionaries. Our Lord is the one who spoke with gentleness and respect to both a learned teacher of Israel and a woman with a questionable past. Our Lord is the one who cared for people's needs, whether making a feast for thousands from a sack lunch or making extra wine at a wedding from jugs of footwash. Our Lord was tempted like us, wept like us, struggled like us, was hungry like us. He said he came to fill us up with joy. And if the Spirit has been at work in our hearts, we do not just know about Jesus, we truly know him. The Jesus we love is our Lord.

"Christ." There is still more: we pray to our Lord Jesus as "Christ." This third word of the prayer is not Jesus' last name. It is a declaration of his place in history. Jesus as Christ is the fulfillment of all God's plans for salvation, from creation to the end of time, from Jerusalem to the ends of the earth. Christ, or "Messiah," means "anointed one." In the Old Testament, when people were made kings or priests, they were "anointed": oil was poured on their head. Prophets also were anointed, but by the Spirit. As suffering Israel waited for salvation, the prophets fixed their hopes on an anointed king to rule them, an anointed priest to intercede for them, an anointed prophet to speak God's word to them. Jesus was this anointed one, the Christ they hoped for, though he was not quite what they had expected: Jesus' kingly reign would be spiritual, not earthly. His priestly intercession would mean offering himself to reconcile humanity and God.

Claiming Jesus as Christ balances our frequent claim that Jesus is our "personal" Lord and Savior. True, he is our own Lord and saving High Priest, but more truly he holds these roles for all God's people across the world and back through every generation, all the way to creation. Jesus does not belong to me. I belong to him, along with the countless millions of others who are grafted into him.

"Son of God." The first three words have shown us Jesus as he relates to us: he is our master, a particular human person and the one who fulfills God's saving purposes. Saying "Son of God" shows Jesus in relation to his Father. The human Jesus, whose mother was Mary, had God for his Father. As the church has clearly affirmed since the fourth century, this points us to the mystery of the Trinity: the One incarnate in Jesus is the Eternal Son of the Eternal Father. Speaking to Jesus, we speak to God.

Jesus is, after all, the "name that is above every name" to whom all creation will one day bow (Philippians 2:9-11). He holds all creation together (Colossians 1:15-17). He is truth itself (John 14:6). His name is a word that puts us in touch with *the* Word, the One who was before creation with God and indeed who is God (John 1:1-3). Jesus' birth made this God known in time and space (John 1:14).

This gives us confidence that our praying matters: we do not just speak to a nice person, a hero whose compassion inspires us. The Son of God has always been there to hear us, and always will be there. It also leaves us standing in awe before the majesty and mystery of the Trinity. This Jesus who cares for our needs bends down from a great height. This Jesus makes God knowable, while pointing out that God's essence is beyond our understanding. We can't comprehend that Jesus, his Father and the Holy Spirit are somehow one God. We can only bow and worship. That is good, since a God subject to human definitions would not be worth worshiping.

"Have mercy." With a clear understanding of the One to whom we pray, we turn to make our request: "Have mercy." This is absolutely a biblical prayer: "Jesus, Son of David, have mercy on me!" called the blind man, meaning he wanted to be able to see (Luke 18:35-43). "God be merciful to me, a sinner!" cried the tax

collector (Luke 18:9-14). This has also always been a prayer of the church at worship. In ancient and modern liturgies, we pray the "Kyrie eleison," "Lord, have mercy! Christ, have mercy! Lord, have mercy!"

What is mercy? Mercy is when someone looks to your needs and helps you out of sheer generosity. The first half of the prayer showed us this is what we need: we have no claim to stake before our Lord, the Son of God. We are not entitled to God's help by right, and we have not earned it. We have to ask for mercy—we are in need and we really can't help ourselves. Jesus' help is a gift we can't earn or repay.

Crying for mercy is quite different from trying to reason or argue your way with God. The Bible includes prayers of that kind, too, of course: think of Moses arguing persuasively with God to keep God from destroying Israel (Exodus 32:11-14) or Hannah making a deal, promising to devote her baby to God's service if only she is given a child at all (1 Samuel 1:10-11). Prayer does feel like persuasion at times, and calling out for justice brings passionate feelings; we beg and we plead and we barter with God. Still, the message of the Jesus Prayer is true: when God answers our prayers, it is always a gift of mercy.

"On me." We pray the Jesus Prayer for ourselves; we ask for mercy "on me." This feels offensive to some: we are embarrassed to focus on ourselves too much, or maybe it seems more generous to pray for other people. Still, this phrase of the prayer is important. It puts our attention on our individual relationship with God. This is true whether we think of the Jesus Prayer as making a specific request or as a form of contemplation. It reminds us that God knows us, loves us, hears us and has mercy on us personally. Each of us has a multitude of needs to bring to God in prayer. Praying for mercy on ourselves urges us toward honesty and wholeness.

That is as far as the most traditional form of the prayer goes.

Readers of *The Pilgrim's Tale* know that some add two words at the end: "a sinner." Some find they do not want to include these words, thinking the focus on sin makes the Jesus Prayer unduly negative. It is not part of the most traditional form of the prayer, so it can certainly be left out. Most of the time I do not include it, but it is worth examining.

This also is a biblical prayer. Remember that the tax collector prayed, "God, be merciful to me, a sinner." Jesus praised this prayer, specifically saying that the man went away justified. That is a key term in Paul's theology, where justification is the solution to the deepest problem of human life: our sin before God. Through faith, we find ourselves justified, counted innocent again. The Jesus Prayer asks for God's mercy in every form, but this is our central need. If it reminds people of the need for forgiveness and healing in their relationship with God, then this longer version of the prayer might well be useful. In particular, one could take it up for a season, as in Lent, when the church year calls us to reflect and repent.

Stage three: Into the heart. The goal is for the prayer to carry on quietly by itself, allowing unceasing prayer within the heart. The pilgrim tells of moving experiences at this point: "I sensed a powerful urge to turn inward. The prayer began bubbling up warmly in my heart and I would need peace and quiet to give free rein to this self-igniting flame of prayer and to conceal from these people the outward signs of prayer."

Delightful to think of, but how does this happen? How can the intellect enter the heart? We have made a good start with the body, getting in the habit of saying the words of the prayer. We took a good next step by working with the mind, getting a solid understanding of what we are saying. We can't stay in the mind, though. It is too hard to concentrate at such length, and most say they can't pray the Jesus Prayer with a focused mind for more than a few minutes. That is all right, because the spontaneous self-generating practice of constant prayer is not a matter of the mind, but of the whole person. The start of this journey, I believe, is to bring our bodily habit of prayer, well informed by the intellect, deep into the center of our being. Thinking about the meaning of the words has taken the prayer deep into our minds; now we can relax, still praying as we breathe, still meaning what we say, but without concentration. There is an inner concentration, though, that is not intellectual. It is an attention to who we are and what we bring as we enter into prayerful communion with God. We try to bring God a whole and undivided self, alive from the center of our being, as conveyed by the image of the intellect moving into the heart.

Some struggle with this. They are comfortable with the Jesus Prayer only if they can concentrate on the words, but that is impossible after a few repetitions. As one put it, "I found my mind wandering, even though my voice was repeating the words out loud." He was frustrated, but it was a first hint of something he might have hoped for: unceasing prayer continuing in the background while he gave his conscious attention to the business of living. The true stillness of the Jesus Prayer with the mind in the heart is far more than initial explorations can bring. I make no claim to having

In the end I felt that the prayer arose and was uttered in my mind and heart by itself, without any effort on my part. Not only in a watchful state but also in my sleep the prayer carried on in precisely the same way. Nothing interrupted it or stopped it for the briefest moment, no matter what I was doing. My soul thanked the Lord and my heart melted away in unceasing gladness.

THE PILGRIM'S TALE

experienced it in its fullness, much less to be able to describe it adequately. Even within a short time, though, the words of the Jesus Prayer can begin to take on a life of their own, so that they do seem to come up from inside, unbidden.

In North American society, people seem to live either in their "minds" as rational people or in their emotional "hearts." The Jesus Prayer is leading us to a more integrated life in the presence of God: the mind comes into the heart, and we pray. Rather than saying or thinking about the words, they flow automatically and we dwell in the Jesus Prayer. Whatever we feel in the time of prayer, we are drawing toward God, who is the still point from which all things have come and around which they all revolve. We find we are standing in the presence of God. The prayer is our breath, and breathing is prayer.

POTENTIAL TROUBLES

A lot of Christians have objections to even trying the Jesus Prayer. Certainly, it is not for everyone; of course, my view is that no single approach to prayer is right for everyone. Often, though, what comes out as a theological objection is really distrust of the unfamiliar. I would not want anyone to stop short of trying this prayer because of false information or prejudice, so let me comment on the objections I hear most often.

One good friend tried to warn me against the Jesus Prayer, saying it might make me go crazy. He had read *Franny and Zooey* by J. D. Salinger (1919-2010), in which a bright young woman became fascinated with *The Way of a Pilgrim*. The Jesus Prayer, my friend said, drove Franny to a nervous breakdown. Personally, I suspect that if someone shows signs of mental illness after praying the Jesus Prayer, they were on the way there with or without it. (Actually, in Salinger's story, Franny downed two martinis on an empty stomach. She passed out on the way to the restroom and spent the rest of the story in misery. Franny did not have a breakdown; she had a hangover.)

To others, the pilgrim's experience with the Jesus Prayer may sound suspiciously like non-Christian forms of meditation. Some ancient and modern Eastern meditation practices teach new recruits to meditate by saying a word over and over again to quiet their minds. These can be names of deities—and of course Christians should not pray to other gods—but the Jesus Prayer does not focus on anyone but the biblical God revealed in Christ. The Jesus Prayer should bring no fear of idolatry. Others note that Eastern meditation practices often work to empty the mind, saying Christians should instead fill their minds with the Word of God. Such critiques often misunderstand both Eastern and Christian meditation. One should not assume that all Eastern meditation aims at an empty mind or that all Christian experience must directly focus on an encounter with Scripture. In any case, every word of the Jesus Prayer is taken from Scripture.

We can find things in common between teachings on the Jesus Prayer and practices in other religions. Praying the Jesus Prayer in a particular posture in rhythm with one's breath has parallels to yoga and Buddhist meditation, since these traditions have found useful connections between the body and the spirit. However, a similarity between religions does not discount the validity of either. If it did, Christians would have to stop loving our neighbors, since other religions say we should do so. With the Jesus Prayer, the body is used specifically to help Christians approach Christ in biblical words of prayer.

Still others find saying the Jesus Prayer contradictory to texts of Scripture such as, "When you are praying, do not heap up empty phrases as the Gentiles do; for they think that they will be heard because of their many words" (Matthew 6:7). The passage mentions two problems. First is praying with "empty phrases" or, as the King James put it, "vain repetitions." Even if the Jesus Prayer is prayed repetitively, the phrases are not empty, and the repetitions are not vain. As we have seen, the words go to the heart of biblical faith. The repetitions have value, too, because they help form our hearts and minds to that faith.

This passage prompts a second objection if we think those who repeat the Jesus Prayer are trying to be "heard because of their many words." This is not the motive. The aim is to dwell in God's presence, in humility, love and awe. Actually, Jesus' words apply better to intercessory prayer styles that would argue God into doing what we ask, refusing to take no for an answer.

Some are bothered because saying the Jesus Prayer seems to preclude other kinds of prayer they find crucial. As one woman said, "There ought to be more to it. I should be spending more time in direct praise. I should be spending more time praying for others. I should have more time to lift up my own needs. Shouldn't I?" Should she? The words of the Jesus Prayer can guide us to a range of issues. Praise of our Lord comes naturally, as does thanks. The request for mercy leads to self-examination and confession. If we understand that any answer from God comes as mercy, we have a place to bring all our varying needs.

I find that the Jesus Prayer is also a real aid to intercession, just as a monk taught the pilgrim in the last conversations of the book. Rather than praying "have mercy on me" the monk says, "When we are remembering our neighbor we ought to pray in this manner: *Lord Jesus Christ, Son of God, have mercy on your servant X.* . . . You can offer a prayer like this for your neighbors several times when you happen to remember them."

Sometimes I have quite a string of prayer requests from others. With the Jesus Prayer I name one with each repetition, with every breath. I am praying specifically, bringing their needs clearly to mind. I am also trusting that God knows best how to answer. No matter what I am asking for, the underlying request is for God to be merciful.

POTENTIAL GAINS
Those who get past initial qualms often find many things to gain in this way of praying. Many find their prayer times frustrating

because their thoughts wander. The Jesus Prayer can help us focus during prayer, each repetition gathering our attention back to God—and that makes it a solution to one of the most common challenges of prayer. This is particularly helpful when the Jesus Prayer is playing in the background while your concious mind is bringing up other topics to pray about. One woman paradoxically described her mind "wandering" from attention to the Jesus Prayer, which actually helped her pray in other ways in the forefront of her mind.

Many find that a minute or two of the Jesus Prayer is helpful as they begin any time of prayer. It draws them back to a quiet focus on God. This is not an empty mind, but a focus on God, the inward gaze toward God that is at the heart of Christian understandings of contemplative prayer. Even for people who would never think of themselves as contemplatives, such as those more drawn to intercessory prayer in the evangelical tradition, a practice that draws our hearts and minds to focus on the presence of the God to whom we pray is appropriate and helpful. And if it does draw us back to quiet in the presence of God, it may leave us more able to hear the nudge of the Spirit or to recall an insight God would give us from our study of the Word.

Some learn to pray the Jesus Prayer when they are angry or anxious out of a related desire to be centered. I suspect that this is a spiritually more helpful kind of centeredness than just stopping to take a few deep breaths. Rather than centering us in ourselves, it puts Christ back in the center, and us back in orbit around him. Though feelings are not the goal, researchers have used biofeedback techniques to show that praying the Jesus Prayer causes a particularly profound state of relaxation. The mind can remain peaceful and attentive long after praying the Jesus Prayer.

The greatest gain of praying the Jesus Prayer, though, is that we might actually receive mercy. We have to want what we are asking for. That was one of the points Salinger made in his story about Franny. In her misery, her brother pointed out that all she wanted was the good feelings that the pilgrim told about. Praying this prayer, we leave the content of the mercy up to God. As Evagrios the Solitary (346-399) taught, a prayer that entrusts the details to God is best: "What is good, except God? Then let us leave to Him everything that concerns us and all will be well. For He who is good is naturally also a giver of good gifts. This is how Jesus taught us to pray in the Lord's Prayer: 'Your will be done!'"

At the heart of God's mercy is the invitation to live in his presence in the communion of unceasing prayer. As we pray, we are contemplating the One who is our Lord, rather than our servant; the Jesus known in the Gospels; the Christ who fulfills salvation history; the Son of God, the second person of the Holy Trinity. Asking for mercy, we depend on God for our every need. Breathing this prayer more and more, it carries body, mind and heart to God, to stand contemplating the name above all names, gazing at the mystery and beauty of the One who holds the universe.

For many readers, I imagine this is the most unfamiliar of any type of prayer in the book. Prayer is such an intimate act that a completely new approach can be unnerving. Be courageous. The Orthodox will tell you it is a journey of a lifetime, but even after a week or two, many begin to discover wonders in the Jesus Prayer, and it starts to work its way into their prayer life.

Lord Jesus Christ, Son of God,
have mercy on me.
Inhale, pray. Exhale, pray. Breathe.

Arriving at God's presence,
abiding in Christ,
Soft—Still—The prayer is my breath.

Dwelling there in God's presence
I find the still point
on which the universe turns.

Still at last, remain standing
with God, mind in heart,
heart in body; stand and pray.

PART TWO

PRAYING WITH SCRIPTURE

You shall put these words of mine in your heart and soul, and you shall bind them as a sign on your hand, and fix them as an emblem on your forehead. Teach them to your children, talking about them when you are at home and when you are away, when you lie down and when you rise.

DEUTERONOMY 11:18-19

God is pretty clear in the Old Testament that we are supposed to pay close attention to the Bible. Deuteronomy 11:18-19 tells us to think about Scripture with our heads, meditate on Scripture with our hearts, and talk about Scripture with our kids and presumably with everybody else, pretty much all the time. Getting Scripture that deeply into our lives has a lot to do with prayer.

The Bible can help us find words to say in prayer, and it can help us listen to God. Many people describe prayer as a conversation with God, but for most of us it is more like a monologue. We talk, and hopefully God listens. But what if God had some things to say to us? How would we find a way to hear?

The most straightforward way to listen to God has always been to bring the Bible into the conversation. Since it is God's Word to us, it makes sense to listen there—where God speaks more reliably than in quiet inner voices that can be our own desires and fears in disguise.

The approaches to prayer in this section use the Bible creatively. From opposite sides of the Reformation, John Calvin and Ignatius of Loyola will teach us very different approaches, one nurturing the ability to speak and the other nurturing a listening heart. They are likely to appeal to very different people.

PRAYING WITH JOHN CALVIN

Studious Meditation on the Psalms

I have been accustomed to call this book, I think not inappropriately, "An Anatomy of all the Parts of the Soul"; for there is not an emotion of which any one can be conscious that is not here represented as in a mirror. Or rather, the Holy Spirit has here drawn to the life all the griefs, sorrows, fears, doubts, hopes, cares, perplexities, in short, all the distracting emotions with which the minds of men are wont to be agitated.

In short, as calling upon God is one of the principal means of securing our safety, and as a better and more unerring rule for guiding us in this exercise cannot be found elsewhere than in the Psalms, it follows, that in proportion to the proficiency which a man shall have attained in understanding them, will be his knowledge of the most important part of celestial doctrine.

JOHN CALVIN,
preface to the *Commentary on the Psalms*

He carries his bony frame into his study with a slowness that comes from pain, his skin taut along sharp features. A sickly man, he can ignore his usual assortment of aches and illnesses. Today's wounds are emotional. Again this morning, when he climbed to the pulpit for the service, there was a note waiting for him—personal, insulting, profane. Just when he needed his faculties, his mind was flooded with memories: open hostility from the city council, quieter but more troubling opposition from colleagues in ministry and, of course, the noisy ball game in the courtyard outside the church—only during worship, only to taunt him. The city of Geneva had begged him to come be their minister. Now people were naming dogs after him.

Finally, the best part of his week: a bit of quiet to prepare for Sunday's afternoon sermon. He opens Bibles, Hebrew and Latin, to the book of Psalms. Praying silently for the Spirit's help, he reads the ancient words of King David:

Be not far from me,
for trouble is near,
and there is none to help. . . .
They open wide their mouths at me,
like a ravening and roaring lion.
I am poured out like water,
and all my bones are out of joint.

◉ ◉ ◉

John Calvin (1509-1564) loved the psalms because he found his own troubled life reflected in them. Though he wrote a shelf of books, he generally kept his inner life to himself—except in the preface to his Psalms commentary. Explaining his prayerful study of the psalms prompts revelations about his childhood and family, his conversion and call to ministry, his struggles and opposition as a reformer and theologian. These things come up naturally, because the psalms give him words for them. Studying what David and the other psalmists went through, listening to their prayers, he understood his own experience; their prayers became his own. For Calvin, the intellectual work of studying Scripture was prayer.

STUDY AS PRAYER

Some remember Calvin as the strong-armed Reformer of sixteenth-century Geneva, praising or blaming him for his influence on Western culture. Many know him as the second-generation Protestant theologian, the systematizer of Luther, Zwingli and others. He had so much to say on more controversial topics that few remember him as a teacher of prayer. But prayer was at the heart of his spiritual life and his theology. For Calvin, prayer is the central thing Christians are called to do, the true expression of authentic faith.

The lengthy chapter on prayer in his *Institutes of the Christian Religion* is a remarkable treatise in itself, synthesizing the full range of biblical teaching on the topic and answering real human questions. Like many books on prayer then and now, the chapter answers every question except how to actually do it. For that, Calvin believed you should look to the psalms—the best teachers on this most important topic.

He spent a lifetime learning to pray with the psalms. One early publication included paraphrases of a number of the psalms in French. He put them into rhyme and meter so his congregation could sing them in worship, making them the whole church's prayers. And praying the psalms in song eventually became a hallmark of Reformed churches worldwide.

The text for his sermon in the Sunday afternoon service was regularly a psalm. He lectured on the psalms to his theological students. Then, in the quiet of his study, he wrote a commentary on a single psalm, not knowing quite why he did it. He liked the result so much that he wrote commentaries on a few more. He showed them to friends, and they encouraged him to write still more. Eventually these became hefty volumes of scholarly and, to Calvin's thinking, prayerful meditations on all 150 psalms.

Neither the psalms nor Calvin's commentaries give up their lessons on prayer easily. The psalms teach by example. Most of the Bible speaks in God's voice or tries to explain things from God's perspective. By contrast, the psalms are the voices of God's people at prayer, crying out to God in all manner of circumstances. And coming inside the cover of the Bible, these human prayers seem to have God's own stamp of approval. They are not, however, organized by topic. Calvin comments verse by verse, so insights on prayer are scattered throughout. He finds more than twenty lessons on prayer in just the first half-dozen psalms.

His only approach to a summary is in the preface. He points to several particular kinds of prayer the psalms teach us. The crucial one is what I call "prayer as mirror and megaphone." The psalms show us our own experience as in a mirror, and then they put a megaphone in our hand so we can speak to God about that experience. This is what Calvin meant when he famously called the psalms an anatomy book of the human soul. In the psalms he saw overflowing joy, rapturous praise, awe and reverence, peaceful stillness, but he also saw boastful pride, brokenhearted depression, vindictive rage and lonely abandonment. As biblical prayers, the psalms invite us to include this full range in our own prayers. God wants to hear even the feelings we are ashamed of, the words we would never speak to another human being. The psalms give us a profound invitation to be completely honest, completely open in prayer.

The psalms, as the soul's complete anatomy, also teach us how to ask God for what we need—the very familiar sense of prayer as petition or request. The psalmists constantly call on God to rescue them, to forgive them and to meet every other kind of need. Though many Christians hesitate to ask God for help, Calvin says the psalmist's willingness to ask was "an infallible proof of his faith." By bringing God our needs and those of others, we show that we trust that God hears and cares and answers.

Thanks and praise are important, too, and the psalms teach these things best. Thanks and praise are not optional: the psalms command us emphatically and repeatedly to "praise the Lord!" though they do far more than repeat that phrase. They list God's good qualities and gracious acts in enormous detail. This is at the heart of healthy prayer. As Calvin says, any prayer that is not side by side with praise of God is just "clamor and complaint." However, he is also emphatic that the psalms teach the grittier sides of prayer and its purposes. He listens to the psalmists struggle in prayer, raging and complaining, but he notes that they come through to the end, confessing their sins, seeking forgiveness and "bearing the cross" of obedience.

> With my voice have I cried unto the Lord. *[David] here informs us that he had never been so broken by adversity, or cast down by impious scornings, as to be prevented from addressing his prayers to God. And it was an infallible proof of his faith to exercise it by praying even in the midst of his distresses.*
>
> COMMENTARY ON PSALM 3:4

FINDING CALVIN'S WAY:
SCRIPTURE AS PRAYER

The problem comes when people try to pray as Calvin teaches. Finding his wisdom on how to pray takes work: we have to take up the practice of studious meditation he models. His psalm commentaries are examples of Calvin's practice of prayer, but I have to admit that at first glance they look more studious than prayerful. He starts his work on each psalm with a paragraph summarizing its message, often linking the psalm to a particular moment in Old Testament history. Next, he translates a few verses from the Hebrew. Finally, he explains the verses line by line, in a paragraph or several pages. He defines difficult words, explains points of grammar and considers how the historical context shapes the meaning. He connects the details to the psalm as a whole, and relates the psalm to the big picture of the Bible as a whole. Still, Calvin is more than just an academic: he constantly draws connections from the text to the life of faith. He is convinced that we are all living the same spiritual life as the psalmists, so the text really can teach us. But is this really prayer?

Yes. For Calvin, study of Scripture can't take place apart from prayer—and when the text is the psalms, study is itself a form of prayer. Calvin taught that human beings are helpless to find their way to salvation without Scripture, which functions like a pair of glasses to put God's message into focus. But if we study the Bible without the presence of God's Spirit, we are basically reading in a dark room—even glasses will not help. Sure, we can study rationally and learn the facts, but we will not hear God's Word to us unless the Holy Spirit comes to shed some light. With the Spirit's illumination, we understand it and know that it is spoken to us personally, with God's own authority. So godly study of the Bible starts with prayer for the Spirit to "illumine" our darkened minds and continues hand in hand with the Spirit as we seek to find what God is saying about our salvation. We are listening to God in the text in the presence of the Spirit and bringing our own lives into the conversation. That sounds a lot like prayer.

Calvin did not lay out a series of steps to help us do this ourselves. With apologies to the Reformer, I will. Many in his tradition and outside of it would benefit from a way of prayer that invites them into the psalms—and to a deeper engagement with Scripture in general—but to get there we need some user-friendly tools. I will look at three different approaches. Though they can work as three big steps in one process, each of them by itself faithfully embodies aspects of what Calvin did when he explored the psalms as prayer.

1. Hearing the text: Learning to study. The first approach is simply the study of the biblical text while praying and as an act of prayer—careful, analytical questioning of the text in the company of Holy Spirit. What Calvin does in prayerful study is not really his own invention. As a child of the sixteenth century, he made use of the tools of Renaissance scholarship, but the roots go much deeper into Christian history. Though Calvin had little positive to say about monasticism, the roots of his practice go down into the medieval monastic practice of *lectio divina*, or sacred reading. Benedict instructed his monks to spend hours each day in *lectio*, as it is often called, prayerfully reading Scripture to listen to God.

Neither Calvin nor the medieval monks would recognize what people today call *lectio divina*, in which a text is read two or three times and people listen for a word or idea that moves them. That is more like a verbal Rorschach test than *lectio divina*. A better sense of the practice comes from a classic medieval text, *The Ladder of Monks*, by a Carthusian prior, Guigo II (d. ca. 1188). Guigo describes four distinct spiritual disciplines, all using the text of Scripture. *Lectio*, or reading, and prayer are treated separately, but the fourfold process is such a well-rounded, prayerful engagement with Scripture that in-

||||||||||||||||||||||||||||||||||||||||||||||||||||||||||||||||

[David], therefore, teaches us by his example, that as often as we are weighed down by adversity, or involved in very great distress, we ought to meditate upon the promises of God, in which the hope of salvation is held forth to us, so that defending ourselves by this shield, we may break through all the temptations which assail us.

COMMENTARY ON PSALM 4

||||||||||||||||||||||||||||||||||||||||||||||||||||||||||||||||

terpreters describe the whole thing as *lectio divina*. Guigo describes the four steps under the metaphor of food: "Reading [*lectio*], as it were, puts food whole into the mouth, meditation [*meditatio*] chews it and breaks it up, prayer [*oratio*] extracts its flavor, contemplation [*contemplatio*] is the sweetness itself which gladdens and refreshes." If we take each one as a separate activity, it is easy to imagine how it would take several hours.

Is this study? A serious intellectual engagement? Or is it something more touchy-feely? Look at Guigo's first two definitions:

> Reading is the careful study of the Scriptures, concentrating all one's powers on it. Meditation is the busy application of the mind to seek with the help of one's own reason for knowledge of hidden truth.

Study defines the starting point of authentic *lectio divina*, and it takes all our energy. Then, having worked to understand the text, we meditate on it—and that also engages our reason. Medieval meditation is often portrayed as rumination, repeating a biblical text inwardly like a cow chewing its cud. For Guigo, it is this and more: we work on the text with active curiosity, breaking it into words and phrases, drawing connections from the text to the same words elsewhere in Scripture, trying to unfold its inner meaning.

He also describes the process of reading and meditation with the metaphor of winemaking: Reading puts a sweet grape into your mouth, but then "wishing to have a fuller understanding of this, the soul begins to bite and chew upon this grape, as though putting it in a wine press, while it stirs up its power of reasoning." Or again, it is like scaling a building: meditation "does not remain on the outside, is not detained by unimportant things, climbs higher, goes to the heart of the matter, examines each point thoroughly." Meditation "takes careful note," "perceives," "thinks." Guigo says the text has to be "hammered out on the anvil of meditation"—a far cry from sharing the word that jumps out at us.

In Calvin's commentaries on the psalms, he practices a very serious *lectio divina* of this kind, but he never gives us a guidebook to teach us how to do it ourselves. Guigo gives us a fine four-step model, but still there is an obstacle: most people do not know how to study. I have been to countless Bible "studies" in which the text of Scripture is never really analyzed for deep understanding; the Bible serves instead as a springboard for personal sharing. Surveys show how seldom many Christians even read the Bible; I tremble to ask how many think hard about the theology of a passage in light of its grammar, history and geography. I suspect that, to those who do not know how to go about it, the idea of really studying a passage of the Bible sounds either boring or intimidating.

> Heal me, O Jehovah. *And this is the order which we must observe, that we may know that all the blessings which we ask from God flow from the fountain of his free goodness, and that we are then, and then only, delivered from calamities and chastisements, when he has had mercy upon us.*
>
> COMMENTARY ON PSALM 6:2

Actually, studying a psalm in a time of prayer can be energizing. As we read and re-read and then read again, asking questions and looking for answers, the Scriptures prove to be an endless source of new insight. The trick is learning how to do it. What we need is a Bible, a good set of questions and time. I also strongly recommend following Calvin's lead and bringing along a pen and some paper. If we write down our observations on the text, even a sentence or so for the questions we ask as we dig into the text, we will end up producing our own little commentary on the psalm like Calvin did—though surely much shorter.

Calvin once quoted Augustine, who said, "I count myself one of the number of those who write as they learn and learn as they write." He was on to something. Writing about something forces our minds to consider it more carefully, leading to better understanding. We make some decisions and take some risks, and the result is learning.

There is no need to try to produce something polished. No one else ever needs to see it. The process of writing down our thoughts is helpful though. When I do this with a psalm, I try to write a one-page commentary in my journal, summarizing what the text I have studied is about. At the end, I find I know that psalm better than I ever have before. And all along the way, by asking specific questions, I find new insights popping up and deepening my encounter with God. Recently when I was praying Psalm 23, I stopped and wrote about the grammar in my journal:

> "The Lord is my shepherd," says the psalm. It is in the present tense. It is not that "The Lord *will be* my shepherd" in the future, meaning that right now all I can do is wait for it to be true, and be patient. Nor does the text say, "The Lord *was* my shepherd," in the past. I do not need to grieve that it is over now, and God is no longer caring for me, looking wistfully back to when God seemed closer or more caring. No, God *is* my shepherd *right now*, today, in my current circumstances.

That may not seem like a particularly deep insight, but it made a difference to me that day—and it came only because I was studying.

So pick a psalm, and set aside a little time to study it. Pray for the Spirit to bring light and insight, and remind yourself from time to time that the Spirit is there with you. Read through the psalm a couple of times, and then start asking questions. If this process is new to you, use the questions in figure 4.1. I recommend taking one question from each category. Read through the psalm, looking for the answer to a question from the first group, and then write down what you discover. Then move to the second category, read, look, and write again. By the time you have worked through the categories, you will have stretched your study muscles.

Of course if you are already comfortable with study, you can just go for it on your own. However, people who are not confident about studying Scripture tell me that using these questions, probing the text for answers and writing out their comments leads them to a richer engagement with the text and to deeper insight. Over time, you will likely also find that the words of a psalm you study remain with you, giving you a vocabulary for your own praises, requests and laments. You may also find yourself hearing God whispering something to you through that psalm. All of that happens because the process really is prayer; through the text of the Bible, you are interacting with God.

2. *Speaking the text: Listening with your life.* The process of study outlined above may feel more like homework than prayer. It does take practice, and it is work. It is also prayer. However, turning to the second approach, we come to something that may *feel* more like prayer.

We may be eager for our side of the conversation. Calvin's approach assumes, though, that we still have trouble talking to God. We may have theological objections: What could a mere mortal say to the all-knowing Creator and Ruler of the universe? How could someone guilty of sin speak, when God's holiness is like a consuming fire? Or we may fear we will bring up the wrong things, or do it in the wrong way. The psalms give us what we need here, too, but only after we have studied them. We have listened to a psalm, asking questions and trying to describe the text accurately in writing, and now the prayers of ancient Israel can begin to be our own. But the psalms will become our prayers only if we can see our own lives in the experiences of the people who first prayed them.

To get there, at least to get there the way Calvin did, we need

Figure 4.1. Questions for Studying a Psalm

1. Begin by describing the psalm.

- Is it short or long?

- Who is speaking? An individual? A congregation? God? An enemy?

- If there is a sense of dialogue, how does it flow?

- If the psalm tells a story of some kind, what is it?

- What sections, patterns, repeated terms, refrains or other structure do you see?

- What do you see in the poetry? Which lines repeat or contrast?

- What subject, topic or theme do you find?

2. Look up unfamiliar words, places or events in a Bible dictionary or concordance. How does what you find change your understanding of the psalm?

3. Describe the outer and inner situation the writer of the psalm seems to be facing.

- What life circumstances are described or implied?

- What emotions does the psalmist seem to be feeling?

- What does the psalmist seem to think are the causes of these things?

- How do the writer's emotions or circumstances change in the psalm?

4. Describe what the writer of the psalm says, or seems to think, about God.

- What actions of God are described? What does this imply about what God is like?

- How is God's character or personality described?

- How would you characterize the psalmist's relationship to God?

- What kind of response does the writer hope to get from God?

5. Describe what the writer of the psalm says, or seems to think, about people.

• What does the writer say about other people's actions and motives?

• What generalizations does the writer make about what people are like?

• What does the writer have to say about his or her own motives and actions?

6. How do your discoveries here relate to what you know from elsewhere in Scripture?

• What other passages affirm the same things?

• What passages point in the opposite direction?

• What echoes of this psalm do you find in the Old Testament? The New?

• Describe any connections you see between the psalm and Jesus' life and teaching.

7. Summarize what this psalm teaches you about one of the following:

• What does it show about the kinds of topics allowed in prayer?

• What does it show about how to praise God?

• What does it show about how God wants us to live?

• What does it show about how people of faith handle hardships?

• What does it show about the nature of the life of faith?

There is no need to work through all these questions. Not all of them are relevant to every psalm, and some overlap each other. But if you look for an answer to one from each category and make the effort to write it down, you may hear the psalm with new ears, understanding it better—or differently—than ever before. Notice, though, this process does not include reading published Bible commentaries. Commentaries are useful, but depending on them makes the process too easy—it can mean letting someone else study for you. Here the task is to do your own study and to write your own commentary.

to return to the psalm, listening to it with our lives. If we studied prayerfully, we probably already found our heart's issues bubbling up. Now this becomes the main focus. Once the text and our life are in conversation, the psalm gives us words to frame our requests, our praises and our self-revelations. As God's Word, the psalm may also begin to ask us questions, inviting us to answer in prayer in our own words.

The range of experience and emotion in the psalms really is striking. Some sing God's praise for the wonders of creation and others moan about the depths of despair. Some look back on God's help through personal crises or national history. Sometimes the psalmist feels persecuted and other times he clearly wants to do a little persecuting. If we begin to ask questions of ourselves, listening for memories of when we have faced or felt something similar, echoes emerge just as

> O my God! my soul is cast down within me. *And, assuredly, if meditation upon the promises of God do not lead us to prayer, it will not have sufficient power to sustain and confirm us. Unless God impart strength to us, how shall we be able to subdue the many evil thoughts which constantly arise in our minds? . . . And, therefore, it is not without reason that David, after a severe conflict with himself, has recourse to prayer, and calls upon God as the witness of his sorrow.*
>
> COMMENTARY ON PSALM 42:6

they did for Calvin. Some days the psalm we meditate on may give voice to what our soul is currently singing, whether a song of joy or a dirge of lament. Other times the psalm may make spiritual sense of something in our past, a season in which we felt abandoned or a time we now realize we were rescued. Still other times we may not be able to connect the psalm to our experience at all.

That should not stop us: even if we have not felt persecuted or depressed, we know that other people have. If we think in expanding circles from our family, through our church and all the way out to the world we see in the news, we can let a psalm lead us to pray for others who experience everything it describes.

The psalms pointed Calvin specifically to the life of David, since tradition said David wrote many of them. As he meditated on the prayers of the psalmist, scenes from David's life came to mind, and all of this reminded Calvin of his own experiences. This allowed him to pray the words of the psalm as his own prayers, speaking to God from a deep place where he felt connected to the Bible and the people who first prayed these words.

We, too, may find the psalms giving us words to pray, or we may find them working like a lens for seeing our lives differently. Finding our experiences echoed in the situations and emotions of the psalmists, we see them from a new perspective, and we find ourselves ready to pour our own words out to God. Either way, study of this "anatomy of the soul" has invited us to bring God all the things we discover when we listen carefully to our lives. The psalmist's experiences have made us more conscious of our own, and the psalm draws us into prayer.

To make this happen, I recommend building on study by reflecting on questions like those in figure 4.2, and writing at least a sentence on one from each pair. Take the one that seems most fruitful and pray a bit further on it, either in writing or in silence. Of course, this prayerful meditation may well lead us to say in some cases, "I have never felt or faced anything like this!" That is no problem; surely another question will prompt us to say, "That is exactly what I'm feeling!" or "I remember when my life was just like that!" If we make such a connection, we can pray the words of the psalm about our feelings and experiences, or we can hold on to the topic the psalm brought up and pray in other ways.

On the other hand, if we come up dry on these connections,

this can lead to further prayer, in writing or in our hearts. We might talk to God about why we have not had such feelings or experiences or why we do not remember them. If something of the psalmist's experience is missing in our life, should we thank God for preserving us from it? Or is it something we should ask God to bring us, some blessing or opportunity for growth? Or are we unable to see our lives in psalms because we need God to open our eyes and soften our hearts? That also is good material for prayer.

These first two exercises—speaking the text and hearing the text—may look something like what is found in daily devotional books. Lots of books and pamphlets of devotions are published, and many people read them, but I always feel they keep me on the surface, a spectator watching someone else encounter Scripture and pray. If we write about a psalm ourselves and reflect on how it connects with our own experience, we go much deeper. We encounter the Word, listen to God and bring our life into the dialogue of prayer.

3. *Singing the text: Translating Psalms into poetry and song.* Alas, not everyone is fond of writing commentaries. In one group to which I presented this idea, some of the more creative participants suspected that Calvin had little to offer them. Then I reminded them that he published some paraphrases of psalms for singing. He rewrote them so that they rhymed and followed the meter of songs. Others completed the French Psalter, and soon Calvin's colleagues across Europe developed metrical psalters in other languages. Singing psalms became the hallmark of the corporate worship of the Reformed tradition. And, of course, what we sing in worship is for many the most heartfelt form of prayer. I encouraged those in the group to do the same: take a psalm and "translate" it into a different kind of poetry and song. For many this was fruitful—both fun and challenging. To put a psalm into a new poetic form requires us to know it very well; we have to study it.

First, we have to explore how the poem gets its ideas across. Un-

Figure 4.2. Listening with Your Life

Present

- In your present life, what *situation* is most similar to what the psalmist is facing?
- In your present life, where are you *feeling* most like what the psalmist is feeling?

Past

- In your past life, what *situation* was most similar to what the psalmist is facing?
- In your past life, when did you *feel* what the psalmist is feeling?

Others

- Who do you know who faces a *situation* like that of the psalmist?
- Who do you know who *feels* something like the psalmist is feeling?

Community

- What in your *church or fellowship* reminds you of what is described in the psalm?
- What in your *community or nation* reminds you of what is described in the psalm?

World

- Who can you imagine, in *another country or another part of society*, who might *face* what the psalmist faces?
- Who can you imagine, in *another country or another part of society*, who might *feel* what the psalmist feels?

like many forms of English poetry, the psalms were not written in
rhyme and meter. Hebrew poetry comes instead in structures of parallel lines. Sometimes the lines repeat and rephrase ideas for emphasis, as in Psalm 51:1-3. Notice how the message of the first half of
each verse (A) is repeated in the second half (B) but in new words:

(A) Have mercy on me, O God, according to your steadfast love;

    (B) according to your abundant mercy blot out my
       transgressions.

(A) Wash me thoroughly from my iniquity,

    (B) and cleanse me from my sin.

(A) For I know my transgressions,

    (B) and my sin is ever before me.

In each case, the second line restates the point for emphasis or
nuance. As we look more closely, we see further complexity here.
If you divide each line of verse one into two parts, (A) and (B) are
actually mirror images:

(A1) Have mercy on me, O God,

    (A2) according to your steadfast love;

    (B2) according to your abundant mercy

(B1) blot out my transgressions

The first half of one line matches the second half of the other,
and vice versa. Sometimes instead of reaffirming the point, the
second line provides a contrast, as in Psalm 20:7-8:

(A) Some take pride in chariots, and some in horses,

    (B) but our pride is in the name of the LORD our God.

(A) They will collapse and fall,

    (B) but we shall rise and stand upright.

In both verses, part A is essentially about "them," contrasting with part B, about "us." On the other hand, there is another kind of parallelism in the two verses: verse seven is about what the two parties cling to, and verse eight is about how things will turn out for them. There are many variations, but the more we listen to the parallel structures of the psalms, the better we hear what the poets were trying to say.

Once we have understood the poem, the translation task is to rebuild it, keeping the ideas intact but expressing them in new patterns. The words we put down must capture the essence of another person's thoughts, and we must also craft something beautiful. That is hard enough, but to do this in a way that sings of our own spiritual experience requires meditation and reflection; we still have to bring our lives into conversation with the text.

Putting a psalm into new words makes it much clearer that we are the ones who are praying, as we see in Martin Luther's hymn "A Mighty Fortress Is Our God." He was actually paraphrasing Psalm 46. He changed it a great deal to express his own prayers in the midst of his struggles, but the psalm is still clearly there underneath the hymn. Calvin and his colleagues stuck a good deal closer to the biblical text in their metrical psalms, but they put the text into the mouths of ordinary Christians, making them tools for and teachers of prayer.

We can rework a psalm into modern free-verse poetry or a classic form like a sonnet, a haiku or a series of them, or even a limerick. Most people I have seen try this have kept the results to themselves, but I have also known some who tried to create something their churches could sing. No matter how we do it, we must discern the message of the psalm and distill it into something new—our own prayer to God.

CONCLUSION: HEARING FROM GOD
ALONG THE WAY

Many find the process of meditative study breathes fresh air into their experience of prayer. Some may be like a bookish woman I know who was more comfortable writing than speaking; Calvin gave her a model that immediately felt familiar. Others may identify with another I know who always struggled in school. However, when she was given questions to guide her study, she could push for answers and find new excitement and insight praying psalms.

Even if these approaches are more elaborate than you want over the long haul, I hope you will invest some energy in trying them out. When prayerful study becomes a habit, the process is instinctive and the formal steps can melt away. When I am alone in prayer with my Bible and my journal the process comes naturally, and it helps me pray with my mind as well as my heart. Study leads to reflection, and by the end of a page I am writing about my life or the world—some situation that the psalm has reminded me of and that I want God to listen to.

The real gain, more than particular insights about a text, is the encounter with God. This is prayer; communion with God through Scripture prompts both speaking and listening. Calvin said of prayer in general that we "call him to reveal himself as wholly present to us." Here Scripture is the meeting place, the very place God intended to speak and be known. Note well, though, that it may not leave you with a *feeling* of having encountered God. It is more likely to feel like the time Moses wanted to see God's glory: Moses was held back, hidden in a cleft of the rock, while God's glory passed by. When he looked out, he did not see God's presence; he saw God *had been* there. Praying the psalms is like that. We return to study and meditate on them day after day, making their words our own. Eventually we look back and notice, "Hey! God was there!"

It is nearly over. He has always been sickly, but now he is so tired, so weak. He is only in his mid-fifties, but today they had to carry him to and from the pulpit. Soon he will have to take his leave, say goodbye to colleagues in ministry and the civic leaders. This is not retirement. He has worked himself to death.

He looks back on trials, yes. True, the work is unfinished. Much good has also been done, thank God. He knows his writings will live on, especially his Institutes and Bible commentaries. But there is a better legacy: so many ministers trained, so many churches planted back in his beloved France, and Christian community and living faith encouraged among the people of his exile home, Geneva. It has been a rare privilege to watch as the gospel has been rediscovered, taught and lived across Europe. He has given his life to the gospel cause.

So much gratitude. All the good is because of God who blesses and guides, who protects, who comforts. Lying in his bed, prayer comes without effort. He calls out to God in ancient words, and yet his own—the rhyming version of Psalm 46 he wrote years ago for his congregation in Strasburg to sing:

Our God you are our firm protection
Stronghold, fortress, and our comfort;
You are indeed in our vexation
Present refuge, and best home port.

Praying with
St. Ignatius of Loyola

The Prayer of the Senses

The persons who receive the Exercises will benefit greatly by entering upon them with great spirit and generosity toward their Creator and Lord, and by offering all their desires and freedom to him so that his Divine Majesty can make use of their persons and of all they possess in whatever way is according to his most holy will.

A colloquy is made, properly speaking, in the way one friend speaks to another, or a servant to one in authority—now begging a favor, now accusing oneself of some misdeed, now telling one's concerns and asking counsel about them.

ST. IGNATIUS OF LOYOLA,
The Spiritual Exercises

Discerning God's will is serious business. You are sure that God must have specific ideas about what you should do. The choice you make may shape the rest of your life: to follow this career or that one; to marry or remain single; to have a child, or another child, or not. Or you may have to make choices that affect other people in your work or ministry. Which path does God want you to follow? How can you know?

Many count on direct input from God for every little decision. Listening for the Holy Spirit's whisper can lead people in strange ways. I have seen someone make a specific life choice because *God said to do it*, only to change direction two weeks later when the experience was different than expected. Did God change his mind? Or was the divine voice actually the person's own? When we ask for guidance I wonder if God wants to say, "Why don't you start with what I told you already? Start with the Ten Commandments. When you have those down, I'll let you know what's next." But we do long for more particular guidance. In Scripture, God gave it—at least when it really mattered. If God wants to have a say in my life, and if I want to do God's will, how can I hear God's voice?

BRINGING OUR QUESTIONS TO GOD

St. Ignatius of Loyola (1491-1556) developed ways of praying that are intended to help us bring God our questions and hear God's answers. He especially wanted to make sure we were not deceiving ourselves by what he called "disordered affections." Ignatius is most famous as founder of the Society of Jesus (commonly known as the Jesuit order) in the Catholic Church, but at heart he was a spiritual director. He helped people discern God's will and see God's activity in their lives and the world around them.

Ignatius got to that ministry the hard way. He was a soldier, aiming for earthly glory, when his leg was shattered by a cannonball. In an age before anesthetics, he endured surgery to set the bone, and when it did not heal properly, he ordered them to operate again—rebreak it and reset it. That should convince you that he was a tough guy. It also tells you he had some time to spend recuperating and pondering what he would do with the rest of his life. He prayed, looking hard at his life and meditating on the life of Christ. In the process, he heard God's calling in a powerful way—the order he founded had a global impact for the gospel. His own prayerful meditations evolved into his Spiritual Exercises: a program for a four-week guided retreat to help people bring their questions to God and hear God's answers.

Working through Ignatius's whole program is a very large project. It still can be done today under the guidance of a director in an intensive month-long retreat. Or, if one can't take a month, Ignatius explains how to do it over a much longer period, taking an hour or more each day to do an exercise. That is well beyond our purpose here.

Ignatius taught a great number of ways to pray in the Exercises, and Ignatian teachers regularly extract individual approaches to use in particular contexts. We will focus on two that can be combined in a healthy discernment process even apart from a guided retreat: "the examination of conscience" or "examen," and "the prayer of the senses." Both are ways of praying with Scripture. As I was writing the chapter I was practicing these myself, and I include some of my journal entries on my experience.

THE WISE COACH

The closer I look, the more I'm struck with Ignatius's graciousness, his wisdom, his kindness. The first section of the Spiritual Exercises is twenty pieces of advice for retreat directors. I'm praying some of the exercises, not leading them, but this is lovely stuff. For instance, he advises directors to fight the temptation to

give too many detailed instructions: people on retreat do not
need to know more about the exercises; they need to pray them.
Ignatius trusts the person who is praying. People will surely find
deep delights and rich insights by their own explorations. All
this leaves me feeling good about Ignatius. He clearly has my
best interests at heart. He wants me to draw close to God and
find God's will.

Ignatius compares the spiritual exercises to physical exercises
to strengthen and train the body. This is training camp, and Ignatius is the coach. He defines his exercises as "any means of preparing and disposing our soul to rid itself of all its disordered affections and then, after their removal, of seeking and finding God's
will in the ordering of our life for the salvation of our soul."

There are two separate processes here. First, the "disordered affections" need attention: sin has messed us up inside, and so we
want the wrong things. Ignatius's examination of conscience
teaches us ways to look hard at our inner lives through a biblical
lens so we can begin to work on corrections. This new clarity helps
us figure out what we really need to ask God about so we can take
the second step and "seek and find God's will." Ignatius's "prayer of
the senses" teaches us ways to bring our questions to God and
ways to listen for answers, all through a prayerful engagement with
Scripture. That makes sense because God's Word is where we most
expect God to speak, a standard to weigh all promptings and inner
voices. These ways of praying combine, first to focus our attention
on our life in Christ and the decisions we face and then to enable
us to ask God's guidance, hear it and follow it.

In Ignatius's time, people went through the exercises to discern
God's calling in a big way—like whether to become a member of
the Society of Jesus. There was a time when people found the Jesuits to be an extreme and scary movement (they were even officially
shut down for a time) but Ignatius's advice to retreat directors re-

veals a wise and gentle spirit. He tries to make sure what they did was helpful for genuine discernment. It would be so tempting to nudge the person on retreat (or "retreatant"; also known as the "exercitant," meaning the person doing the exercises) toward the commitment the director thinks is best; it would be a great way to increase the numbers of the Jesuits. Ignatius nips this in the bud: the retreatant has come to hear God's will, not the director's, so the director must stand back.

Ignatius trusts that God will speak, and that people at prayer really will listen. He is flexible, adapting the retreat for those who are poorly educated or intellectual, spiritually advanced or immature. The retreat's four "weeks" are more stages than periods of seven days. They can be made shorter or longer as needed—in the second week he includes twelve days' worth of plans.

Directors are to take particular care when the retreatant is in a vulnerable place. If someone is filled with joy, on a spiritual high after a moving day of prayer, it would be easy for them to jump into a major life decision. Or an unstable person might take vows to enter an order—and the church would expect them to keep their vows—even if sober reflection showed that was not really God's call. Better to hold them back, keep them doing all the exercises, so they really hear God. Ignatius never acts like a sales agent pressing to close a deal. He wants people to hear God and answer, and that takes time. He has them return to Scripture and prayer again and again, getting past self-deception.

THE EXAMEN: LISTENING TO YOUR LIFE

I just did the "examination of conscience" and actually it was not such grim work. Ignatius doesn't want people to obsess on this. He recommends pondering each Commandment (or sin or virtue) only for as long as it would take to say the Lord's Prayer and the Hail Mary three times. On my watch that is just shy of two minutes. So I spent a half hour taking stock of my life, and it was kind of freeing. Normally I plow forward through life, assuming or asserting my innocence. I give myself the benefit of the doubt many times a day. I really do want to grow, but I'm usually a little vague on the details. Now I have a great deal of clarity. I end this time of prayer with two Commandments and two "cardinal sins" that I could use some effort on—where daily attention could make my life more like Christ wants it to be. Having clear direction feels light, not heavy.

Ignatius puts a lot of weight on prayerfully looking at our own lives. He sees it as a necessary step toward bringing our questions to God in prayer. Without self-examination, our disordered hearts would have us asking the wrong questions—or we might not know what to ask at all. We will look at three different ways to practice the examen, two directly from the exercises and one from modern interpreters of Ignatius.

The first is the "general examination of conscience," which is done prior to making formal confession. Ignatius encourages us to thank God, ask God's help and then think through our lives "hour by hour or period by period," considering ways we may have strayed in our thoughts, our words or our actions. He wants us to look hard for where we have kept and disobeyed each of the Ten Commandments. He also has us look at our lives in light of the "seven capital sins" (pride, anger, avarice, gluttony, lust, envy and sloth) and their corresponding virtues (humility, patience, generosity, temperance, chastity, neighborly love and diligence). We consider these things with careful psychological analysis, looking at ways we have misused our memory, our intellect and our will. The key, though, is that this is prayerful self-examination with Scripture, whether it is the Commandments or the vast biblical teaching that informs the vices and virtues. It sounds like a lot, but it is not intended to be exhaustive or obsessive. A couple of minutes on each topic is all he suggests.

This may have been familiar stuff to late-medieval Catholics, but it's not to twenty-first-century Protestants. We are fine with a general, corporate confession in worship, but tally our individual sins? We retreat behind fears of "works righteousness" or "neurotic guilt." We do not really want to know. Personally, I have come to trust Ignatius. I am also convinced that he is right: the Commandments really are good, and the deadly sins are deadly. Looking hard in the mirror is necessary to moving forward with Christ and crucial to becoming clear about what my questions are.

Bringing life into prayerful conversation with the Ten Commandments and other passages of Scripture will leave anyone aware of at least one issue that needs work to live as God calls us to. That awareness is just what we need to see the value in the second form of the examen, the "daily particular examination of conscience." Here we are not trying to reform our whole life all at once. We pick that one thing we know we need to work on, and we pay attention to how we are doing on it. Ignatius has us make a chart something like figure 5.1, with two lines for each day of the week.

Every day we are to go through three steps: When we wake up, we pray for help on the chosen issue. At noon, we think back over the first half of the day, counting the number of times the problem behavior came up. We mark a dot on the top line of the current day for each occurrence. Before bed, we look back on the last half of the day and add any necessary dots to the bottom line. Then we can look back at the chart, looking for improvement. Fewer in the afternoon than in the morning today? That's good. More today than yesterday? That's too bad. How does this week's total compare with last week's?

A cognitive-behavioral therapist could hardly make a better plan for personal change. Ignatius made this a daily requirement for members-in-training of the Society of Jesus, not just during the retreat. I suspect he would have liked them to do it always. It

Figure 5.1. The Daily Particular Examination of Conscience

Sunday

Monday

Tuesday

Wednesday

Thursday

Friday

Saturday

sounds overly negative to many people today, but, as with the general examination of conscience, it does help us know ourselves better as disciples, making us aware of the problems and questions we need to bring to God in the prayer of the senses.

In recent decades, writers on Ignatian prayer have emphasized a third form that we might call a kinder, gentler examen. Some rename it "examination of consciousness," which certainly sounds more modern. It also points to something deeper. Igna-

tius's spiritual exercises do not aim at a scrupulous focus on behavior, but a growing awareness of God in all things. Ignatius
called this search for God's activity "discernment of spirits," and
it is the task especially of his retreat directors, who must understand people's inner lives.

In this newer form of the examen, we focus on the task of discernment by examining what Ignatius calls the "motions of the
soul"—the inner nudges that draw us toward God or away from
God. He calls these tuggings "consolations" and "desolations,"
things that give a sense of the gracious presence of God or the
seeming absence of grace, the absence of God. This is less a way of
praying with Scripture than the other two versions of the examen,
but it is perhaps even more helpful in preparing us for the prayer
of the senses.

The process is quite simple: we give thanks to God and quiet our
hearts to reflect on the past day or week. In God's presence, we
bring to mind both the consolations and the desolations, in prayerful silence or writing them in a journal. We ponder their signifi-
cance. We close with a prayer thanking God for being present in
our experiences, offering ourselves to God anew. This form of the
examen can be done individually or as a gentle, conversational way
to pray with a friend or in a group. It can be especially helpful for
married couples who want to pray together, which many find challenging. It is also a delightful way to deepen prayer with children.

This kind of examen begins to tune us in to God's work in our
midst, since raising the question prompts us to try to find the answer. I know of one church in which the new pastor was committed to this process and began his first meeting with the elders by
asking them, "In the last month, what were the signs you saw of
God's grace?" This was followed by an awkward silence. However,
the question got them thinking. The next meeting opened with
the same question, and some were ready. Soon it became a habit,
and they began to lead the church by watching for God at work.

The practice can also be misinterpreted. People often answer as if the question were, "What made you happy and what made you sad?" Ignatius was not trying to deal with surface emotions. A consolation, as Ignatius used the term, is not something that makes you happy but something that draws you near to God. In Ignatius's words, "I mean that which occurs when some interior motion is caused within the soul through which it comes to be inflamed with a love of its Creator and Lord." A consolation leaves you with more love for God, more faith in God, more hope in God. Such things might be joyful but might as easily include tears of grief.

By desolation, Ignatius specifically meant the opposite: things that "move one toward lack of faith and leave one without hope and without love." These might be very happy things, but things that leave us farther from God: "one is completely listless, tepid, and unhappy, and feels separated from our Creator and Lord." It takes inner quiet to notice the things that have increased our love for God or our faith in God. It takes a particular kind of courage to know or share the things that have eroded trust and hope.

If we nurture our awareness of these things on a daily basis, we really will know what is going on in our relationship with God. After asking these questions for a while and noticing the answers, patterns emerge. From places of persistent and surprising consolation come discoveries of God at work making us new. From repeated desolations come awareness of ways we need to grow and wounds that need healing. Or careful attention to desolations may reveal the underside of grace—that God is present and working even in the darkness. We will know where we have problems or questions, and we will be much more prepared to hear God speak.

Whichever way you choose to try it, the examen can be a rewarding kind of prayer. After a week of practice, one woman exclaimed, "Finally, prayer can actually be about me!" That was not narcissism. She was juggling seminary courses and family responsibilities as well as pastoring a church. She took the spiritual responsibility of ministry very seriously, carrying her people before God daily. Pouring her life out for others, she risked burning out. Praying the examen gave her room to nurture her own relationship with God.

God invites each of us to walk in a relationship of love and trust, and in the examen we bring ourselves into conversation about that relationship. Prayerfully reflecting on our lives in light of Scripture and the traces of grace allows the conversation to deepen and flourish, building awareness of God's action and our own needs for growth.

THE PRAYER OF THE SENSES:
BRINGING YOUR LIFE TO SCRIPTURE

I'm thinking the exercises of the first week are not what made Ignatius popular. He does teach me to use my imagination and senses here, but mostly that has meant getting a complete vision of hell—including the smells. Okay, okay, I am much more aware of the consequences of sin!

Still too many dots on the lines of my little examen chart, but I press on.

I like the second week better. I have read the story of the Annunciation countless times before, but Ignatius's "application of the senses" gives me a richer awareness of the scene. Visualizing Mary's house showed something different from the Renaissance paintings in my memory—meager furnishings, a few things for daily sewing and cooking. Conjuring the smells of a first-century Palestinian village puts the scene in my gut rather than my head.

Once we have looked prayerfully at our lives in conversation with Scripture, we probably have some things to talk to God about. Maybe we had questions already, but they might not have been the *right* questions. The examen can make us rethink our questions, turn them around a bit and clarify them—and that makes it much more likely we will find useful answers. With our question in hand, we are ready for Ignatius's most fascinating prayer practice: he called it "the prayer of the senses" or the "application of the senses." We meditate on a biblical story using our imaginations to experience the text with all our senses, finally entering the scene imaginatively and conversing with the characters. As we bring our whole selves to both Scripture and prayer, Ignatius gives us a way to bring Jesus our concerns and actually listen for his replies.

The process has several steps. On an Ignatian retreat, we would be given a passage of Scripture, typically a Gospel narrative, and would spend several hours prayerfully studying it throughout the day. We would pray for God's help, review what we learned in our study and call to mind the question we need to ask God. Then the application of the senses: we would pray through the text several times, each time imagining what one of our senses would experience in the scene. That is, we would first go through the story with imaginative sight, then hearing, then taste and smell, and finally touch. To use our senses, we would have to be inside the biblical scene, so part of the process is to imagine ourselves among the characters. Then, deeply immersed, we would speak to the people, and especially to Jesus, bringing our question. Finally, we would listen to what they say in response.

This makes praying with Scripture also a way to listen to God. Without Scripture, we can have trouble knowing whether the voice we hear is God's or our own. But to make Scripture a place for prayerful listening to God, we have to do something different than many of us do. For some, the devotional reading of Scripture means reacting to a text with our emotions, but Ignatius wants us take the text much more seriously. People often study biblical texts, but to Ignatius, study is only preparation. This process requires intellectual work and emotional presence—and every other form of engagement a human person can bring. Ignatius's prayer of the senses allows the Word of God to be the forum for prayer as real conversation, asking God questions, knowing we are heard and actually hearing answers.

That is the outline. I want to take one text and flesh it out a bit: the wedding at Cana (John 2:1-11), the scene of Jesus' first miracle. You can do this along with me with your own question in mind. It will work better, of course, when you have honed your question with the examen and then work through the text of your own choosing and the Spirit's prompting. But this will give you a sense of how to go about it.

The first step is to spend some time getting to know the text. If possible, follow Ignatius's advice to study the wedding at Cana prayerfully, but at least read it a few times so it is fresh in your memory. Consider where it falls in the flow of the Gospel. Get to know its outline and actions. Think on what it shows about Jesus and what it implies about God's purposes. Listen to what it teaches you personally. You might take your journal and write about the lessons the passage teaches you. Then we will be ready to do the prayer of the senses together

We start by coming to God in prayer, ready to speak and listen. This means placing ourselves in a right attitude before God, making it clear to both of us that our goal is to better love and serve God. As Ignatius put it, "The Preparatory Prayer is to ask God our Lord for the grace that all my intentions, actions, and operations may be ordered purely to the service and praise of his Divine Majesty." Continuing in prayer, we remind ourselves and God of what we are coming to talk about;

> *The Preparatory Prayer is to ask God our Lord for the grace that all my intentions, actions, and operations may be ordered purely to the service and praise of his Divine Majesty.*
>
> THE SPIRITUAL EXERCISES

we bring to mind the text and the lessons it taught us.

Our first journey through the narrative is trying to "see the persons, by meditating and contemplating in detail all the circumstances around them." In our imagination, with the text open before us or by memory, we picture what our eyes would see moment by moment. See it in vivid detail. Who would be at the wedding? The text tells us of Jesus, Mary, disciples and servants. Who else do we see? Biblical narratives are very lean, and there are always details left out—things that simply must have been there. Look beyond the words to see these too. Clothes are not mentioned, but what would people wear to a first-century wedding in Galilee? Is the celebration inside or outside? What furnishings do you see? What is the light like at this time of day? Are people standing or sitting, talking or dancing?

This is not an empty exercise: at every step Ignatius wants us to benefit, "drawing some profit from the sight." Surprisingly often, we do benefit. The imagination brings details into view that would never come up through standard exegesis, leading to insights and new perspectives. When I get to the place where the wine has run out, I "see" a lot of people gossiping, criticizing, laughing—and making sure the host can't see them doing it. When I see those six huge stone jars of water, I get a sense of a wealthy household and a courtyard. These and other details give depth to the story and set a tone in my reading. It does not matter if that can be verified by historical exegesis; it is about my imagination, and my prayer.

Then we go through the text again, applying our sense of hearing. Using our imagination, we "listen to what they are saying or might be saying." That is, if there is little explicit dialogue, we need to listen for unrecorded conversation. Listening to words spoken in the text, we try to hear the tone of voice, the volume, the emotions carried between the lines. Then we listen to the environment: What are the sounds of this place? Is there music at the wedding? Speeches? Are there animals around? Are there other sounds from the neighborhood? Again we ponder these things and draw benefit from them. I hear dishes clanking, feet scraping and a roar of background conversation. Listening to the tone of people's voices, I hear Mary's kindness in her concern for the host and her confidence in her son. When water becomes wine, I used to think the steward was praising the host. Now I hear bewilderment and frustration that the groom didn't bring out the Dom Pérignon *before* all those cases of Chateau Jordan Embankment.

We go through the scene again with the senses of smell and taste. In one exercise, Ignatius mentions tasting the "sweetness and charm of the Divinity," but there is much more for these senses, even if the passage is silent about it. Comb through the story again, start to finish, once for each of these senses. Clearly, there is wine—at least by the end—but there must be interesting food to smell and taste. There is probably dust, and bodies too—perfumed or rarely washed? Farm smells are probably not too far away. The bitterness of shame is in the mouths of the steward and bridegroom when they realize they miscalculated. I smell sweat as servants carry thirty-gallon jars of water. Even if I do not gather a clear lesson from this, the process takes me still deeper into the biblical story, adding feeling and engagement.

By this point Ignatius intends us to find ourselves fully inside the story. In one example he says, "Using the sense of touch, I will, so to speak, embrace and kiss the places where the persons walk or sit." Exploring the text with the senses forces us to be there. The question is, who are we? Maybe we take on the role of a named character, or perhaps we are a servant or guest. What do we feel in our bodies as we walk through the narrative? Are our feet dusty in sandals? Is our stomach full of food? Is our throat dry from wedding chitchat? Is our back sore from hauling miraculous wine? What does each character likely feel in her or his body? What do we do, physically, as we participate in the story?

Imagination moves us from intellectual study to something more experiential. Without trying too hard, we make vivid, interesting observations. The process invites us to something deeper, though, when we move to the final stage. Ignatius calls it the "colloquy." As we are fully immersed, he tells us to talk with the people in the scene. In our assumed role, we come to Jesus—or Mary, a disciple, the steward, anyone. We ask the question we brought to the exercise. And then, still in the story, we listen for what Jesus or another character says in response.

Ignatius's plan has been to get us deeply involved with the events of the gospel, face to face with Jesus himself. We are not studying these stories in an intellectual exercise. We are fully engaged, drawing close intellectually, emotionally, even physically—and so, spiritually. We are ready to ask, ready to listen in the presence of the one who can answer. That is a fertile situation for prayer. And we are praying, with Holy Scripture as our guide for the journey. Once they get into it, some can carry on a whole conversation.

A colloquy is made, properly speaking, in the way one friend speaks to another, or a servant to one in authority—now begging a favor, now accusing oneself of some misdeed, now telling one's concerns and asking counsel about them.

THE SPIRITUAL EXERCISES

However, we should not assume that we have heard a direct word from God, even if the exercise brings a rich and vivid response. Really hearing God requires discernment, and that takes place over time, in an ongoing dialogue with prayer and Scripture. We need to return to the text to listen again; then we bring our question to another text, and another. We must weigh today's word alongside what we know of God, Christ and Scripture as a whole.

I find this is a natural part of the process. Engaging with the stories keeps the prayerful conversation active, and discernment happens as I live with the responses. I keep listening, noticing whether this word lives on with conviction or rankles against what I know of God, Scripture or myself. Remember that Ignatius had his directors hold people back from jumping to decisions. They continued through the whole month, applying their senses to text after text.

OPPORTUNITIES AND CHALLENGES

Each time I do the Prayer of the Senses I like it more. Even if this is not "study," I find new insights—sometimes it is just the feeling of the text, but sometimes I understand the meaning differently, or more deeply. The trouble comes at the end, when I bring my question to Jesus. I am fully in the story, but when I come forward to talk about my question, it falls flat; I hear no response. I think I'm too watchful, too afraid of self-deception.

Still I gain something. I do not generally hold back my questions and complaints in prayer, but this approach feels less like I'm hurling my cries into the darkness. Feeling myself in the scene, in the presence of Jesus, I have a sense that I have been heard.

Some who have the freedom (or whatever the mysterious quality is) to enter the conversation find that God does speak. I suspect that people can make this more likely to happen if they write out the imaginary dialogue, taking the exercise as far as they can in their journal. But others, without imagining the words of response, find their question or problem reframed as they engage with a passage of Scripture so fully. Either way, there is the sense that God has spoken. Clarity comes; the guidance they longed for has arrived.

This can have a profound impact. One single woman in her forties prayed through this story of the wedding at Cana. For single adults, weddings can be hard places to be, but she entered the scene, imaginatively sensing her way through the text. She came up to Jesus. Whatever her question was, she asked him—and Jesus asked her to dance. She knew this was not scholarly exegesis; men and women probably would not dance together at an ancient Jewish wedding. What she heard was still "true" in terms of being authentic. Her real self was interacting with the real God, the conversation facilitated by Scripture. Theologically, it was very deeply true that Jesus loved her, not in a general way, but personally. Jesus wanted to sweep her off her feet.

Other people's experience, including my own, is quite different. We enter the text imaginatively, we approach Jesus, and we ask our questions—and then, nothing. Not conversation, but silence. This may be a sign of an underdeveloped imagination or a more rationalistic personality, but it does not feel disappointing. What we really want is to be able to communicate with God. Even if we do not hear lots of dialogue, we do feel that we have been heard—and that is enough. It is a gift to use every part of our selves to move closer to Jesus in prayer.

The greater challenge is integrating this type of prayer in daily life. One woman who thrives on Ignatian prayer wanted the prayer of the senses to be a daily discipline, but it took more quiet, focused time than she could find. Occasional personal retreats provided what she needed. She could do the examen regularly, becoming aware of God's activity and her questions. Then, in twenty-four hours at a local convent, she could use the prayer of the senses to have a rich experience with a biblical text—and God spoke powerfully. She would come away with a renewed relationship with God and a clearer sense of what God was doing and saying.

No matter what I say, some think this whole process is too touchy-feely. I hope, though, that you will at least experiment with it. Your imagination is no less a tool of God's creation than your reason. Your theology may be rooted in scholarly exegesis, but this is not about doctrine. This is a way to foster a genuine conversation, fully engaged with God's Word.

On the other hand, if you find rationalistic approaches like Bible study dry, academic and empty, here is an invitation to use other parts of yourself. Ignatius shows a way to find life in the Word—finally a way to approach Scripture that is lively and prayerful, dialogue rather than dogma.

If the prayer of the senses leads you to hear from God, the message will not be something out of the blue. If it is God speaking, it will be true to what God already said in Scripture. You are going to hear what God has been trying to say all along, whether an affirmation of God's forgiveness or of a whole new life direction. You are just more likely to hear it because you figured out the right question and brought your whole self to ask it—and you asked it in the place God has always been speaking.

CONVERSATIONS, LIGHT AND DARK

The Lord said to Moses, "Come up to me on the mountain, and wait there." . . . Moses entered the cloud, and went up on the mountain. Moses was on the mountain for forty days and forty nights.

EXODUS 24:12, 18

Thus the Lord used to speak to Moses face to face, as one speaks to a friend.

EXODUS 33:11

The three types of prayer in this section focus on our side of the conversation. We turn toward God and then—what? Moses himself seems to have gone two opposite directions, sometimes engulfed in a dark cloud and other times talking so intimately with God that he shone with reflected glory. Unlike the ways of prayer in the earlier sections, in these chapters the conversation is not shaped by any preformed words or mediated by Scripture.

And unlike those in the concluding section, here we are not necessarily asking God to do something. Here prayer is primarily about being with God, whether we converse in our own words or contemplate in silence.

Each of these ways of being in communion with God is completely different from the others. The written prayer practices of the Puritans contrast strongly with the spontaneous inner conversation taught by Teresa of Ávila, and both are radically different from the wordless silence taught in *The Cloud of Unknowing*. All are ways that prayer happens when we, frail children of dust, stand face to face with our Maker, Defender, Redeemer and Friend.

PRAYING WITH
ST. TERESA OF ÁVILA

Recollection of the Presence of God

Take my advice, then, and let none mislead you by showing you any other road than that of prayer.

Speak with Him as with a Father, a Brother, a Lord and a Spouse—sometimes in one way and sometimes in another, He will teach you what you must do to please Him.

ST. TERESA OF ÁVILA,
The Way of Perfection

When I teach on prayer, I sometimes do a little survey of how people currently pray. At the top of the list: conversation with God. They talk with God in the car, in the shower, at the store—even in my classes, apparently, when they should be paying attention.

Many who pray this way are influenced by *The Practice of the Presence of God* by Brother Lawrence of the Resurrection (c. 1605-

1691). It is an unusual book. Actually Brother Lawrence never sat down to write it—he was far too humble for that. Instead, people who knew him collected summaries of conversations with him, letters he wrote and sayings he liked. He was a French Catholic, a Carmelite monk, but Protestants of all stripes read him and admire his wisdom. Brother Lawrence tells how he made a radical commitment to being constantly aware that God is near; this bubbles over into "a continual conversation with Him, a conversation free of mystery and of the utmost simplicity." It is a classic way to follow Paul's instruction to pray without ceasing. However, to some the whole idea seems almost irreverent. How can people chitchat with the Ruler of the universe enthroned in majesty, surrounded by flaming angels who cover their eyes in humility? As the late John R. W. Stott allegedly once said, "God is not your Cosmic Chum!"

And yet.

Prayer, in any form, contains this same crazily unequal, unimaginable, impossible situation: the creature is invited to talk back to the Creator, the sinner to commune with the Holy. How can the finite stand in the presence of the Infinite? This is the nature of prayer. Some are struck silent in awe; others chatter away about every little thing—a fact that makes the awestruck feel a bit queasy.

PRAYER AS CONVERSATION

Though I favor communion with God as a definition of prayer, people commonly think of prayer as conversation. It is an imbalanced conversation: whether imploring God for mercy and forgiveness, crying out in lamentation or asking for a miracle, prayer is usually our speech to God. Thankfully, Scripture not only invites but commands us to speak to God, even if we know that in a real conversation we must also listen.

This tells us something about the gospel. In a radical action of grace, God chose to bend low and dwell among us, and still bends down to listen. This choice reveals God's true nature: the awesome and mysterious God loves us personally and sacrificially. Prayer is possible, not because we are worthy to reach up to God, but because it is God's nature to reach down to us. Even now, after Jesus has returned to heaven, he wants to know us, to understand our experience, to hear us.

The casual style of such open conversation with God makes it seem very modern, but it has its roots in older traditions, especially in the writings of a Spanish nun, St. Teresa of Ávila (1515-1582). Teresa was the reformer of the Carmelite order and its most important teacher on prayer. Brother Lawrence was her student a century later, a great example of her teaching in action.

Even if we are already able to talk to God easily and openly, Teresa has a lot to teach us. She works from biblical ideas about God rather than from today's human-centered individualism. That is, she invites us to a free and open conversation with God, not because we are personally free and open people but because of who the Bible says God is. She can also help those who are silenced by the paradox of talking to God, since she offers simple, practical tools to spark the conversation.

TERESA AND "RECOLLECTION"

Teresa joined the Carmelites, a Catholic order devoted to the contemplative life, but—as the Protestant Reformers were quick to point out—in the sixteenth century, monastic life had fallen from its ideals. This Carmelite lived as a socialite, leaving the convent to visit around town. God grabbed hold of her, though, and in a series of visions, she became convinced that Christ was calling her to reform her order.

In that era, women were held down by male authority; a woman claiming direct guidance from God could end up before the Inquisition. Still, Teresa spent the rest of her life heading the reform movement, eventually in partnership with a Carmelite monk, St. John of the Cross (1542-1591). Through her influence, many came to devote themselves more fully to Christ in lives of prayer and holiness. She was declared a Doctor of the Church in 1970 (one of only three women ever so honored) because of her writings on prayer and the dynamics of the spiritual life.

Teresa is best known for the book *The Interior Castle*, a brilliant exploration of the transforming experience of intimacy with God. In another book, *The Way of Perfection*, she is more practical. She wrote it as a manual for her nuns, to shape their characters and their practices in a life devoted to Christ. At the heart of that life, she teaches, is prayer. She describes a number of ways of praying, and distinguishing them from each other is part of her genius. They amount to successive steps in the path to true spiritual maturity, union with God. This chapter will focus on just one, something she describes with unique clarity, though it has earlier roots. Teresa calls it "recollection," and it comes fairly early in the journey.

The term *recollection* has two meanings. In a formal definition Teresa says, "It is called recollection because the soul collects together all the faculties and enters within itself to be with its God." This is closely related to what today is often called "centering" in prayer. When our inner lives become fragmented, we take time to re-collect them. But the examples she gives of how to do it amount to something quite different: it means calling to mind or "recollecting" one of the Bible's portraits of who God is: king, father, bridegroom and so forth. Each biblical picture puts us in a different relationship to God, and we focus our attention fully on it.

This is a powerful tool to spark prayerful conversation. Just as we speak differently to a head of state, our parents and our spouse, concentrating on God in particular biblical roles prompts different kinds of words. Different kinds of interaction flow in different relationships. Since Teresa directs us to the biblical revelation of God, she prompts prayer in the most reliable, least superficial way.

To see where recollection fits in Teresa's teaching, we need to understand her spectrum of types of prayer. She starts with the most basic way of praying, which she calls "vocal prayer." She means what people might call "saying your prayers," reciting written prayers as any nun or monk would do, including some form of the divine office. This was already a requirement, and clearly some thought they had fulfilled their obligations by rattling off the liturgy. Teresa tells them they can't stop there; they must move on to "mental prayer." That is, when their mouths are reciting a prayer, their minds must be at work too; when you pray, you have to mean what you say. Her example is the Lord's Prayer, and she spends a large part of the book explaining it. She tells her nuns that they should take a good hour to pray it mentally, and even then they may not get through it all. The key is to be fully engaged. As she puts it, "Do not, I beg you, address God while you are thinking of other things."

The opposite end of the spectrum, as the title of her book indicates, is "perfection." She does not mean perfect outward obedience, as if flawless behavior were the requirement for salvation. The late-medieval Catholic knew, though, that some kind of perfection was possible. After all, Jesus said to be *perfect* as God is *perfect* (Matthew 5:48) and told the rich man that if he wanted to be *perfect*, he should sell all his possessions, give the money to the poor, and come follow (Matthew 19:21). The church called all the "religious"—meaning the nuns, monks and priests—to follow the "counsels of perfection," which included Jesus' command of poverty as well as requirements of celibacy and obedience.

Teresa means a perfection that goes beyond this. Jesus' word, which we translate as *perfect*, really refers to reaching a goal or end. She understood the goal of the spiritual life as union with God. Teresa wanted all her nuns to be united with God in love, which she sometimes called spiritual marriage. Contemplative prayer is at the heart of such union, so contemplation is at the far end of her spectrum of ways of praying. While some kinds of contemplative prayer are "acquired," meaning that we can take them up and practice them by choice, the form Teresa aimed for is different. The contemplation that embodies union with God happens to us only by God's action. She called it "infused" contemplation to make sure we know it comes from outside ourselves. It is a pure gift, transforming the inner life of the one who receives it.

Infused contemplation should be understood as a rare experience. I have known a number of people who describe rapturous experiences, using language similar to that of Teresa. However, Ruth Burrows, a modern Carmelite interpreter of Teresa and John of the Cross, notes that we should not deceive ourselves about union with God. It is internal but, if it is authentic, it leads to external change. A real connection with God can't fail to make us more loving in relation to our neighbors. Experiences, however moving, that leave us with a sense of our own superiority and specialness are not the real deal.

Recollection comes much earlier, toward the middle of the spectrum, but it is connected both to mental prayer and to contemplation. Actually, Teresa's descriptions of recollection and mental prayer are sometimes so similar that the definitions blur:

> When you speak, as it is right for you to do, with so great a Lord, it is well that you should think of Who it is that you are addressing, and what you yourself are, if only that you may speak to Him with proper respect. How can you address a king with the deference due to him, or how can you know what ceremonies have to be used when speaking to a grandee, unless you are clearly conscious of the nature of his position and of yours?

Here she is discussing how mental prayer is necessary for real vocal prayer, but to explain it she gives a solid example of recollection. To engage our mind with the meaning of the Lord's Prayer, Teresa has us recollect the role of God as king. Sometimes, as if trying to make things confusing, she also talks about recollection in relation to infused contemplation—but like infused contemplation, such recollection is from God, not an action on our part. Some of the confusion comes from her writing style: Teresa makes for challenging reading because she uses terms in varying overlapping senses, and she spirals around her ideas rather than walking straight through an outline. Still, the core teaching on recollection is a powerful tool for nurturing a well-grounded conversation with God. Master it, and we are left inwardly directed toward God in the first steps of acquired contemplation.

GETTING STARTED

The best way to make sense of this practice is to look at Teresa's advice, then consider her examples and try them out. First, the advice. When she suggests we look at a biblical portrait of God or Jesus, she is not suggesting we study and analyze. As she puts it, "I am not asking you now to think of Him, or to make long and subtle meditations with your understanding. I am asking you only to look at Him." Teresa's distinction between thinking and looking is key. She is trying to spark intimacy, not scientific description.

Who can say that it is wrong if, before we begin reciting the Hours or the Rosary, we think Whom we are going to address, and who we are that are addressing Him, so that we may do so in the way we should? . . . For we cannot approach a prince and address him in the same careless way that we should adopt in speaking to a peasant or to some poor woman like ourselves, whom we may address however we like.

THE WAY OF PERFECTION

When we think, we evaluate, draw conclusions, discern principles and patterns. We are in our heads, with God under our microscope. Looking is different: it is about presence and relationship.

She is a contemplative, and contemplation is about looking toward God with what she calls "the eyes of your soul." We look at the One who loves us, and this draws us into relationship. Looking at a biblical portrait of God does not require us to become biblical scholars. Her examples include prominent and traditional New Testament portrayals of God and Christ, as well as some that are a bit less familiar.

King. One prominent image is that of lord or king. As we have seen, this leads her to ponder the respect and honor one must show to people in high office. But she also takes courage because this great King has bent low and invited us to speak. She has no patience with those who think humility means silence: "A fine humility it would be if I had the Emperor of Heaven and earth in my house, coming to it to do me a favor and to delight in my company, and I were so humble that I would not answer His questions, nor remain with Him, nor accept what He gave me, but left Him alone." We only honor and obey our sovereign Lord if we speak out in prayer.

So, as we sit in prayer, we look with our soul's eyes at the God of heaven and earth, enthroned in glory. The God we look at is in charge of all that happens to us, in us and around us. This is the King of kings and Lord of lords, the guide and goal of all history. This Ruler has come near and invited us to speak. So speak: what is on your mind? We might well be impressed and burst forth in praise. We might remember blessings received and pour out our thanks. If we feel oppressed, we might humbly ask for justice. Remembering wars and famines, we might seek mercy and peace. See what issues come up and what words come out when you sit with the King.

Father. If talking to the Sovereign of the universe is intimidating, Teresa's other images are more comfortable. Jesus taught us to pray "Our Father," inviting us into his own relationship with the first person of the Trinity, and Teresa considers this role at length. Probably more than people in our culture would, she emphasizes that having God as our Father encourages us to speak humbly. But even in the patriarchal world of sixteenth-century Spain, she knew that a child draws near to a father for help and comfort. So it is with God. We must "ask Him for things as we should ask a father, tell Him our troubles, beg Him to put them right."

She does not want us to think of a faraway, austere father. We need not shout to be heard. As we cast our gaze toward God as Father, we remember that he is right there with us: "However quietly we speak, He is so near that He will hear us: we . . . have only to find a place where we can be alone and look upon Him present within us."

So we cast our gaze, not on the human father who raised us (helpful or unhelpful as our parents may be in knowing God), but on the Father of Jesus who adopts us as beloved children. If God is our Father, responsible to love us, raise us and provide for us, what do we want to say? Perhaps we have needs that a father should provide: food and shelter, work and relationship, and many other things. Perhaps the bullies of our neighborhood have been hounding us; we need our Father to defend and protect us. Perhaps, as a little child does sometimes, we just want to sit close and have a cuddle. Picture this Father and see what flows from your lips in prayer.

Spouse. Jesus described himself as the Bridegroom and his people as the waiting bride. From very early centuries, Christians looked at the Song of Songs in the Old Testament through these roles, hearing a metaphor of Christ and the believer in King Solomon's love poem. Teresa and other monastic writers embraced this idea for themselves. Some saw their chaste vows in the convent as a kind of wedding, and some, like Teresa, aspired to a mystical state of spiritual marriage. Her recollection of Christ as Spouse carries particular intensity: "Your Spouse never takes His eyes off you, daughters," she writes. "See, He is only waiting for us to look at Him, as He says to the Bride." The intensity flows naturally from the nature of the image: a bridegroom's passionate love for his bride.

With this relationship in mind, Teresa turns her attention to the actions of Christ on our behalf—passion again, but with a different meaning. Seeing his suffering prompts the loving bride to cry out, "O Lord of the world and my true Spouse!" because "seeing Him in such a plight has filled your heart with such tenderness that you not only desire to look upon Him but love to speak to Him, not using forms of prayer, but words issuing from the compassion of your heart." It prompts her to ruminate on Jesus' love for her in her brokenness and on the fact that he even wants her devotion: "Art Thou so needy, my Lord and my Good, that Thou wilt accept poor companionship like mine? Do I read in Thy face that Thou hast found comfort even in me?" And it sparks reconsideration of her own problems: "If Thou, Lord, art willing to suffer all this for me, what am I suffering for Thee? What have I to complain of?"

When you approach God, then, try to think and realize Whom you are about to address and continue to do so while you are addressing Him. . . . Why, God save us, when a woman in this world is about to marry, she knows beforehand whom she is to marry, what sort of a person he is and what property he possesses. Shall not we, then, who are already betrothed, think about our Spouse, before we are wedded to Him and He takes us home to be with Him?

THE WAY OF PERFECTION

Teresa's recollection starts with the role of Jesus as Spouse and moves to the memory of what our Spouse did on the pages of the Gospels. If we look hard at Jesus and remember that he is not only the Lord we follow but the Bridegroom whom we marry, we too might find new things to say. That is, while being with a king brings out humble words, with a lover one shares intimate secrets, heartfelt sorrows, joyful hopes. Instead of formal praise, devotion brings words of love. Tender gratitude is different from awe in the face of grandeur. Look to Christ the beloved, the bridegroom, and see what you want to say.

Friend. Other roles come up at least briefly, but I will mention just one more: Teresa recollects the image of Christ as friend. This is not as common in the New Testament as the others discussed, but it is there. At the Last Supper, Jesus told his disciples that they were no longer his servants, but his friends (John 15:14-15). The idea fills Teresa with wonder. Affection makes us want to stay with our friends and makes us want to know them better, so we take every opportunity to be together. She wants friendship with Jesus to motivate us to stay in a state of prayer, where we can speak to him and know him. She calls this to mind as she prepares her sisters to pray the prayer Christ taught, the Lord's Prayer: "Imagine that this Lord Himself is at your side and see how lovingly and how humbly He is teaching you—and believe me, you should stay with so good a Friend for as long as you can before you leave Him. . . . Do you think it is a small thing to have such a Friend as that beside you?"

For Teresa, recollection of Jesus as friend is even a cure for the wandering thoughts that trouble so many in prayer: "O sisters, those of you whose minds cannot reason for long or whose thoughts cannot dwell upon God but are constantly wandering must at all costs form this habit."

This recollection is an early step in acquired contemplation; it is essentially a contemplative stance, dwelling in the presence of God, gazing toward God. Turn your eyes upon Jesus, she might say, look full in his wonderful face. She tells her sisters to "shut themselves up in this way within this little Heaven of the soul, wherein dwells the Maker of Heaven and earth," turning away from what their actual senses perceive.

But the physical eyes can help, too, if you have an icon or other portrait that reminds you of the One to whom you are speaking: it is something "to use regularly whenever you talk to Him, and He will tell you what to say." It becomes a tool for recollection, a conversation starter: "If words do not fail you when you talk to people on earth, why should they do so when you talk to God?" None of this is arduous. Teresa just wants her reader to "make the slight effort necessary for recollection in order to gaze upon this Lord present within her." Much as modern evangelicals speak of inviting Jesus into their hearts, Teresa finds the presence of Christ deep within the heart and soul—and where Jesus is, heaven is.

BROTHER LAWRENCE
Brother Lawrence is the great example of Teresa's prayer of recollection in action. He uses concepts and phrases that make me think he knew *The Way of Perfection*, though it may just be that Teresa's teaching was pervasive in Carmelite monasteries and convents and he simply absorbed it. He clearly thinks of God with love, but he is generally not as explicit as Teresa about the picture of God he is recollecting. Looking between the lines, though, the image of God as friend seems to shape Brother Lawrence's practice more than any other. To this he adds the conviction that God is always the generous provider, the good and wise guide of all things: part of his conversion came when he saw a tree in winter and considered how God would bring it to leaf, flower and fruit. It left him permanently convinced of God's loving providence and care.

Occasionally he does explicitly name this focus on God as friend and providential guide: "We cannot put too much trust in so good and faithful a friend who will never betray us in this world or the next." And again, "You would think it rude to leave a friend alone who came to visit you. Why abandon God and leave Him alone?" His sense that God is his friend gives him the freedom to joke around. When he got in trouble, he prayed, "I shall never do otherwise if You leave me to myself; it is up to you to keep me from falling and to correct what is wrong," or "that is what I usually do when I am left to myself." When he had expected monastic life to be difficult but found it quite pleasing, he prayed, "You have outwitted me." He encouraged people to be open, frank and honest with this divine Friend, taking time to entrust every task to him. He showed this dependence even about things that looked like his own responsibility—when he had a chance to do good he prayed, "My God, I cannot do this unless You enable me to do so."

Method: Decision, recollection, conversation. Scattered through Brother Lawrence's *Practicing the Presence of God* are three consistent basic steps, his own take on Teresa's recollection. The first step, in his own experience and as he teaches others, is to make a clear decision to stay consciously in God's presence. You must "from this very moment, make a holy and firm resolution never to be willfully separated from Him, and to live the rest of your days in His sacred presence." It is commitment without condition, regardless of whether God makes it a happy experience or not.

The second and third steps come together: we recollect that we are in God's presence, and then we let prayerful conversation flow. The recollection is straightforward: "I keep myself in His presence by simple attentiveness and a loving gaze upon God which I can call the actual presence of God." The words of prayer flow directly from the recollection. Actually, to Brother Lawrence, this contemplative gaze, the presence of God, is best defined as "an habitual, silent and secret conversation of the soul with God." The conversation will include all the topics that come up in prayer, but the goal is to "take delight in and become accustomed to His divine company, speaking humbly and talking lovingly with Him at all times, at every moment, without rule or system." The rest of his practice was a repetition of these last steps, whether devoting his day's work to God before beginning a task or returning to recollection if he forgot God for a while. Throughout the day, "we should stop as often as we can, for a moment, to adore God from the bottom of our hearts, to savor Him, by stealth as it were, as He passes by."

If this sounds simple and straightforward, Brother Lawrence would be pleased. Remember, though, that it begins with the great commitment. The first step shows it is actually a very serious approach to prayer; the apparent simplicity of ongoing casual talk with God comes only with a deep and permanent change of inner orientation. But Brother Lawrence says himself that it is not complicated. It is the easiest way he knows—and the only way. The thing is to start, because "everyone is capable of these intimate conversations with God, some more, others less; He knows what we can do. Let us begin."

Further portraits of God. In his letters, Brother Lawrence sometimes describes recollection using portraits other than Friend. These include those used by Teresa, such as King and Father, but some are less familiar. Gazing on God filled him "with greater happiness and satisfaction than that of an infant nursing at his mother's breast; and for the inexpressible sweetness which I taste and experience there, if I dared use this term, I would willingly call this state 'the breasts of God.'" It is a surprising image until you read Isaiah, where God cries out as a woman in labor (Isaiah 42:14) and says it would be easier for a nursing mother to forget her child than for God to forget Zion (Isaiah 49:15). After suggesting that the people nurse at Jerusalem's "consoling breast" and "drink deeply with delight from her glorious bosom," God goes on to say, "As a mother comforts her child, so I will comfort you" (Isaiah 66:11-13).

Brother Lawrence says, "Sometimes I think of myself as a block of stone before a sculptor, ready to be sculpted into a statue, presenting myself thus to God and I beg Him to form His perfect image in my soul and make me entirely like himself." The image of God as sculptor is hard to find in Scripture, though God as potter is found in both Old Testament and New, with at least one reference to the clay speaking back to its shaper. Brother Lawrence seems to boldly take this as an invitation to conversation, begging to be made into the best kind of vessel.

Yet again he urges his reader, "Present yourself in prayer to God like a dumb and paralytic beggar at a rich man's door; concentrate on keeping your mind in the presence of the Lord; if it sometimes wanders and withdraws itself from Him, do not let it upset you; confusion serves rather to distract the mind than to recollect it; the will must bring it back calmly; if you persevere in this way, God will have pity on you." The images draw on a number of Gospel scenes and parables, putting the person at prayer in a clear role with a typical problem. We beggars have to wait attentively for God, the rich person, to come out, but our minds wander. Recollection here will mean gently bringing our minds back to prayerful waiting, rather than getting mad at ourselves or giving up.

Brother Lawrence mentions or alludes to recollection of a number of other portraits of God: God as judge, with himself as criminal; God as doctor, with the praying person in need of healing; Christ crucified; God as host at a banquet; God as consuming fire. All have connections to Scripture, and any of them could be useful in prayer.

MOVING FORWARD

Teresa leaves us with one more portrait of God: he comes to us as guest. Though it may seem to reverse the natural roles, this makes us God's hosts. Teresa's point, expanded to book length in *The Interior Castle*, is that God is not found outside us, but deep within the faithful heart. Our life, our soul as she would call it, is a house, a palace, a castle. The journey of spiritual growth, which is prayer, takes us through it. We start out knowing neither God nor, frankly, ourselves. The more we open up to God in prayer, the further in we go, room by room, until finally we come to our heart, the inmost chamber. We find God is there already.

Teresa is not confusing herself with God. Rather, God made our hearts for himself and comes to the place perfectly fitted for him. Coming to him in prayer, we welcome this divine Guest, and other concerns melt away: "If we took care always to remember what a Guest we have within us, I think it would be impossible for us to abandon ourselves to vanities and things of the world." It draws us to more consistent prayer, to know God better and stay with him: "I think, if I had understood then, as I do now, how this great King really dwells within this little palace of my soul, I should not have left Him alone so often."

For some, the very traditional portraits of God as King and Father present obstacles to prayer rather than resources. If they can't be used, so be it—though time spent in recollection with a loving gaze toward God may, eventually, make them useful again. It is wise, though, to use some scriptural portrayal of God as your starting point, as Teresa and Brother Lawrence did, whether we stick to the ones they recommended or search out our own. Christians worship and obey the God revealed in the Bible; devising gods of our own is strongly discouraged throughout. But neither St. Teresa nor Brother Lawrence exhausts the possibilities of Scripture as a resource for recollection. As we search out ways that God is portrayed in the parables of Jesus and the poetry of the prophets, we will find those that feed our souls and provide fruitful recollection.

If all of this does not sound perfectly natural, leading to an easy and open conversation with God, take a more experimental approach. Each day, set aside a short time, say five to fifteen minutes, to practice in one of these two ways: A first approach would be to take just one of these biblical portraits each day and turn your inner gaze upon God. Gently consider who this God is and who you are as a person before God in this day's particular role, whether Father or Friend or whatever. Listen to your own heart, and speak what comes up, silently within your mind, framing it in appropriate language to speak to God in this role. The next day, try a different biblical portrait.

A second approach would be to start the time of prayer by listening to your heart to know what you want to pray about. Then take several of the portraits of God in turn, spending just a few minutes speaking to God about the same life issue, each time in words appropriate to the particular portrayal of God—first as King, then as Spouse and so on. Beyond this, some people find it helpful to start by writing the words of the conversation in a journal. Whichever method you try, I encourage you to keep at it for a couple of weeks. If you can't do it every day, do multiple sessions spread across a longer period.

St. Teresa and later her disciple Brother Lawrence were transformed by living this life of prayer. Teresa experienced what she called "favors" and "consolations," in the form of feelings of rapture and visions. Brother Lawrence felt such overwhelming joy at the presence of God that he had to work actively to hide it. But such things were not the goal for either of them. The goal is to love God.

That is the good news of prayer. Even if some reach high and holy states that we do not, prayer itself draws us to the presence of God. The act of prayer, especially a form of prayer that helps us turn our attention to God in contemplation and conversation, is very like the definition of heaven. Brother Lawrence refers often to the joy he felt from practicing God's presence, but he notes a more substantial benefit: "Faith becomes more alive and more active in every occasion of our life . . . for the soul, accustomed by this exercise to rely on faith, by a simple act of recollection sees and feels God present, calls on Him freely and efficaciously, and obtains what it needs." The mental act of recollection should make prayer flow spontaneously, but Brother Lawrence encourages us to have some prayerful words at the ready, like "God of love, I love You with all my heart." But if a memorized phrase seems awkward, it is fine to use "any such words that love may beget on the spur of the moment."

Who would not want such joy and living faith? Who would not want words to come so easily in prayer? Both of these teachers called the result union with God, and both acknowledge it as God's gift—a sadly rare gift. For St. Teresa, a Doctor of the Church, this kind of recollected conversation is one of many practices on the way to union; for Brother Lawrence it is the whole journey. But Brother Lawrence gives hope to those who do not receive the extraordinary gift: "One can at least . . . acquire by the practice of the presence of God a way and a state of prayer which very closely approaches this simple gaze."

PRAYING WITH THE PURITANS

Meditation in Writing

Now in the next place I shall speak of the manner how such a Journall is to be used.

For observation take notice of these three Rules:

1. Labour by faith to see and observe God in all things that are bestowed on you. . . .

2. Labour by faith to see and observe all these good things in God.

Thirdly, observe well the *mediums,* the choyce wayes and means by which all good things are conveyed to us.

JOHN BEADLE,
The Journal or Diary of a Thankful Christian

Back in student days, after a bad breakup, my journal saved my sanity. I bought a little black book to hold my dark, grieving thoughts, and in it I poured out lamentation, confusion and anger. I wrote, and wrote, and wrote, until I didn't need to anymore. A couple of years later, I looked back and found that pretty much every page was the same. You could say writing was a kind of therapy, but for me it was prayer. God was listening. Healing came.

I often pray best with a pen. I feel like John Ames, the aged, dying Congregational minister in Marilyn Robinson's Pulitzer Prize–winning novel *Gilead*. The book is Ames's spiritual autobiography, written so that his young son will know him: "For me writing has always felt like praying, even when I wasn't writing prayers, as I was often enough. You feel that you are with someone." Writing in my journal draws me quickly and surely into God's company. God is there, listening, and I find myself understood and accepted. That changes me.

It may seem an odd, indirect form of prayer—I do not start each journal entry with "Dear God"—but if prayer is conversation, the act of writing allows me to take my part of the dialogue seriously. It slows me down, and hidden things come to light. Burdens are lifted. Insights and possibilities emerge.

When I teach writing as a discipline of prayer, those who are enthusiastic typically already practice some kind of journaling. Journaling comes naturally to some, but not to everyone. Others squirm and object, even after being forced to try it out. "It just isn't prayer" is the most typical response. "I hate to write" is a close second. Students and people whose professional lives require a lot of writing can have a hard time breaking out of established forms and styles. Others have hated writing since grade school—put pen to paper and they break out in a cold sweat. To all who resist writing as a way of prayer, I plead for an imaginative openness. A great many people find that writing sparks spiritual growth. Just take a look at the many books published on journaling, whether by Christians or artists or counselors.

The first time I tried to write in a journal, I found myself so anxious I destroyed every page. I was not afraid that someone would see it. The struggle was with myself. Here were my feelings, the insides of me, spread out on a page. I felt almost naked. Later, and to my own surprise, I tried again. Soon writing in my journal was the way to come honestly to God and find grace. All I can say is that it is worth it to keep coming back to the experiment of prayerful writing.

GETTING STARTED, GETTING UNSTUCK— PURITAN TEACHERS

Nothing is a fit for everyone, but if writing itself is the stumbling block, there are ways to get past it. Clear the way, and you may find that praying in a journal has a lot to offer. My high school English teacher set me in the right direction. I had always gotten stuck staring at a blank page, but Mrs. Clark set me free: every class started with five minutes of writing whatever came into our heads. Some just wrote, "I hate writing, I hate writing, I hate writing," until the time was up, but that was fine with her. The pen just had to be moving. She didn't even read it.

That experience shortened the journey from a thought in my head to a sentence on the paper. It is a technique taught in many books on the writer's craft, whether they call it "free writing" or "daily pages." Some say to write for a set number of pages, and others assign a period of time, but the discipline is the same: write and write, without stopping to edit or criticize. Do that for a while, and writing itself may no longer be a problem.

Even if you can write, you still have to figure out what to write about. If this is a new way to pray, that can be a challenge. The good news is that many Christians have prayed this way throughout history.

There is no better example than the Puritans. Now, before you start rolling your eyes, let me say that these sixteenth- and seventeenth-century Calvinists from England and then America have gotten a bad rap. We assume the joke is true that a Puritan is defined as someone terribly afraid that someone, somewhere, is having fun. In literature class we read *The Scarlet Letter* by Nathaniel

Hawthorne (1804-1864) or *The Crucible* by Arthur Miller (1915-2005), and forever after when we hear "Puritan," we picture poor Hester Prynne being judged and shamed, or the horror of the Salem witch trials.

However, if you read what actual Puritans wrote about the Christian life, the picture changes. They brought single-minded passion to their pursuit of God. They lived with a focused, prayerful longing to be made new in Christ. They may have been more conscious of sin than most Christians are today, but they were also more aware of God's blessings and grace. These were inner experiences, but I can describe them confidently because when they prayed about them they often did so with pen in hand. Written approaches to prayer were so important to the Puritans that they wrote manuals to teach each other how to do it.

So how can we actually get started? What we need is a set of role models and a set of tasks to try out in our own journals. We will look at three Puritan works, each one focusing on a different task. I think you will find that with their guidance you really can write, especially if you reframe what they describe in modern terms that fit your needs. Trying out any of these models takes work, but that is true of any new spiritual discipline. It takes practice before the spiritual equivalent of muscle memory can take over.

FINDING TRACES OF GOD: JOHN BEADLE'S
JOURNAL OR DIARY OF A THANKFUL CHRISTIAN

John Beadle (1595-1667), an English Puritan, thought the discipline of keeping a journal was crucial to spiritual growth, but he could find no book on the topic. So in 1656 he wrote one himself, calling it *The Journal or Diary of a Thankful Christian*. He sees a biblical mandate for keeping a journal: God commanded Moses to write down the Israelites' travels (Numbers 33:2), and so we, too, need to keep track of God's faithful guidance. Samuel set up a stone as a reminder that God had helped him thus far on his journey (1 Samuel 7:12), and so we too should mark and remember special times of God's intervention. Writing to discern and remember God's actions in the past or in the present builds faith.

This is obviously a spiritual discipline to Beadle, but is it prayer? It absolutely is intended as a process that seamlessly leads into prayer. His own grateful faith shines through in his writing, winsome and joyful, and he is constant in calling us to thanks and praise for what God has done. The whole process, though, nurtures an awareness of the presence of God, seeing God in all of our lives and seeing all in our lives in light of God, carefully attending to the means God uses to bring about every blessing. This is a kind of contemplation, a gaze toward God mediated by the traces of God's grace in the world.

The Puritans, as Calvinists, had a very hearty doctrine of providence, believing God was actively involved in virtually everything in their lives and the world. Today the idea has fallen on hard times. Many assume God is not actively involved, or they look at things that happen in the world and wonder what God could possibly have been thinking. Providence filled Beadle with a sense of wonder. He claimed that if we only looked, we would see God's name, wisdom, power and faithfulness in every blade of grass and every drop of rain. Nurturing awareness of providence can bring us to awe as well. Believing, as Elizabeth Barrett Browning put it, that "earth's crammed with heaven, / And every common bush afire with God" makes it more likely that we will notice God at work, take off our shoes and kneel. "The rest sit round it, and pluck blackberries, / And daub their natural faces unaware."

Beadle lists a number of topics to write about in our journals. Some are more clearly prayerful than others, but they all help us move forward in seeing God at work and giving thanks, knowing God better and loving God more.

1. "Let every man keep a strict account of his effectual calling." "Effectual calling" is the Puritan term for the way God got through

and made you a Christian. Beadle is suggesting that we write out our spiritual autobiography. We can start with the bare chronology of our Christian journey, whether we were nurtured gently to faith or had a radical conversion. Beyond that, though, we need to fill in the story and look for what God did at each stage to help us believe and then grow. Who were you before? How did you learn of Jesus? What helped prepare you? What obstacles did God overcome to win you? Were there wrong turns or fresh starts? When you really look, how was God at work? Write it all down.

2. "Take special notice of all divine assistance . . . either in the performance of the duties that are required of us, or in bearing those evills that are inflicted upon us." Instead of narrating the past, here Beadle asks us to take note of how God is active in the present. We have Christian responsibilities in relationships and work, and God is there, helping us be faithful. Inner life brings duties, too, and God is working behind the scenes to help us grow. And there are the hard things, challenges ranging from trying coworkers to natural disasters, and God is supporting us in the midst of them. If we take on Beadle's assignment of listing

If your Honors will be pleased to throw away an hour or two in the perusall of these lines, you may be hence encouraged more and more to observe God in the wayes of his providence; and keep some memorials by you of his goodnesse to you and yours; which may much encrease your faith in him, enlarge your love to him, and fortifie your hearts against the evils of these times.

THE JOURNAL OR DIARY OF A
THANKFUL CHRISTIAN

how God has assisted us in the past week or year, we are more likely to notice and give thanks.

3. "Remember, and for that end put into your Journal all deliverances from dangers, vouchsafed to you or yours." Beadle also wants us to take note of more dramatic ways that we are saved from tragedy and attribute the blessing to God. Have you ever come near death by disease or accident? Did God help you through a financial tragedy? Have you been brought safely through broken relationships? What about others in your family? Every day, in ways large and small, God saves us and those we love. Writing these down in prayer, we move from saying, "Whew! Another lucky break" to "God, you were there. You are so good to me!" If we record even some of them in our journals, we will eventually look back at a long list of God's gracious actions.

4. "All the instruments, all the men and means that God hath in providence at any time used for our good, must not be forgotten." Beadle wants us to write about the past as well as the present, looking at the specific people God has brought our way. The great gifts of God come most often through people. If we note them as agents of God's grace, we will be more thankful, crediting both the individuals and the God whose goodness they have shown us. Beadle lists parents, teachers, benefactors and ministers, as well as people in working life. If we make a record of people who have helped us, it is only a short step to seeing God's hand. And if we think about the "problem people" in our lives, we may find that God has used them to shape us as well, prompting a whole new kind of thanksgiving.

5. "And finally, mark what returns, what answers God gives to your prayers, and set them down . . . as most remarkable pledges of his love." Keep a list of what you pray for and how God answers. This is, I would guess, the most commonly recommended kind of prayer journal today, even if it is a minimalist one. It can certainly prompt us to engage more actively in praying for others. When someone asks us to pray, rather than simply saying the words and moving on (or worse, forgetting to pray at all), journaling reminds

us to pray and to watch for God in action. In the process, we build faith and gratitude.

Try one of these tasks in your journal. Ask God to show you the traces of grace in your past and present life. Pray as you write, and go back later to read and pray about what you wrote. What we see and record of God's actions is inevitably shaped by our own theology and personality. But we stand a better chance of seeing by clearer light if we keep coming back, asking the questions and writing about what we find.

TELLING GOD THE TRUTH: THOMAS HOOKER'S
THE CHARACTER OF A SOUND CHRISTIAN

Our second Puritan model of prayerful writing is the practice of self-examination. As well as looking for God's actions in the world, Puritans looked very hard at themselves. They wanted to come honestly before God. We should often take an account of our lives, said Beadle's friend Thomas Hooker (1586-1647), to see what progress we are making in godliness: "For want of this examination, many live and die hypocrites, and know it not, but suppose their case is good." The point was not to wallow in guilt, but to live in truth before God and neighbor. It was not enough to be born again: a Puritan had to grow up again. Whether at the turn of the year, on each birthday or before receiving the Lord's Supper, they took time to examine their lives, often recording the result in their journals.

Writers like Hooker gave readers tools to help in the process. In *The Character of a Sound Christian in Seventeen Markes*, Hooker describes the life of a Christian who is mature and consistent, a disciple to the very heart. In the short work Hooker summarizes Christian maturity in seventeen challenging "markes" or character qualities which we use to weigh and measure our own lives. They become questions we ask ourselves to probe our growth in Christ's likeness. Each of these seventeen topics comes with related biblical texts for meditation, and these can be pondered as we reflect on our lives prayerfully in writing. We are to consider each one in turn, looking inward to see what we see. The process is intended to bring us to want to take new steps of faithfulness in the categories where we see we need to.

In a Puritan's journal, we are more likely to find a summary of such times of self-examination, but I think the process works best if we write throughout. I will mention a few of the marks on Hooker's list; that will be just enough to get the flavor of it, and I'll fill in with some commentary. It can be bracing just to read the Hooker's marks and biblical texts, but writing about ourselves in light of these high standards helps us work through to clarity. The task is to think about our lives in light of the character qualities Hooker describes, and to write a paragraph or more telling God how we are doing in that area. Doing this in the context of prayer should help make it a gracious and useful process. Honesty should lead both to some gratitude for where you have grown and to some repentance and fresh starts.

Mark number 3: "If when thou mournest for the sinnes of the times, thou take heed that thou art not infected with them." It is easy to condemn the world for its sins. Who does not grumble sometimes at the state of society? Hooker thinks a consistent Christian should go beyond grumbling and be sad. That is harder to do, because it implies we are connected to the world, faults and all. We write our way toward his measure of real maturity, though, when we make an inward search for ways that our own lives actually embody the things we complain of.

Mark number 5: "If thou canst chide thy owne heart for the coldnesse and dulness of it to good duties, and use all holy means for quickning it up afterward." Hooker knows that as time passes, passion and zeal can fade. With God, or family, or work, we start well, ready to do great things, only to grow cold to the responsibilities that come with our commitments. Honesty requires we admit the fires need stirring. Hooker's mature Christian does not just feel bad about it, but finds "the means for quickening it up." Pen in hand, we brainstorm things that will restore a growing faith or a loving marriage, the things that will help us bring our best to the work God calls us to.

Mark number 6: "If thou canst be patient under afflictions, and better for afflictions." Do we pretend every day is victory and joy? Hooker's picture of maturity includes admitting we all have troubles. It also requires us to look hard at how we handle them. Do we rage or sulk? Hooker suggests that integrity means growing as a result of trouble. We can list on paper the parts of life in which we need to exercise patience. We can write about any given struggle to see what lessons it might be teaching us or consider what opportunities for growth it brings.

Mark number 9: "If thou art as well content to submit thy heart and life to God' s Word in all things, even when it crosses thee in thy profits and pleasures." Hooker assumes we are encountering the Bible. If we are not, that in itself is something to write about. He assumes we are going beyond learning Scripture's contents and bringing our lives into line with what it teaches. Again, there may be things to reflect on and write about here, but real maturity, according to Hooker, goes beyond the easy stuff. He would have us reflect and write about parts of life in which obedience is inconvenient, costly or unpleasant.

Hooker's language may seem archaic, and taking on someone else's list as your tool for self-examination may seem artificial. If you prefer, do the same with the Ten Commandments. Or do what Hooker himself did, and compile a list of the qualities you think mark Christian maturity, pairing each assertion with a biblical text. You might come up with more than Hooker's seventeen, or fewer, but you would create a standard by which to measure your own growth. But slow down and be clear with yourself about your current inner and outer life. Write to God about where you think

you stand today, or this year, and let God into the process of helping you grow.

MEDITATING ON SCRIPTURE AND CREATION: COTTON MATHER'S *CHRISTIANUS PER IGNEM*

Our third Puritan teacher in the way of prayerful writing is
third-generation Bostonian Cotton Mather (1663-1728). Mather
was an advocate of meditation and wrote a book about it, filled
with all the quirky emphasis of the writing of that era: *Christianus per Ignem; Or, a Disciple WARMING of himself and OWN-
ING of his Lord: With Devout and Useful MEDITATIONS, Fetch'd
out of the FIRE, By a Christian in a Cold Season, Sitting Before It.*
He thought it was a clear duty for Christians to spend fifteen
minutes each evening in a two-part practice of meditation on a
passage of Scripture: "Let the first part be, to *Inform* our selves,
and the second be to *Affect* our selves." The results of this kind
of meditation appear frequently in Puritan diaries, but Mather's
book is actually about another kind of meditation. The Puritans
called it "spiritualizing the creatures," or looking at things in the
world and drawing analogies to biblical teachings on the Christian life. Mather puts it this way:

> All the *Creatures* of God about us, are so many *Preachers*
> from God unto us: . . . As there are *Footsteps* of the Divine
> *Power*, and *Wisdom*, and *Goodness*, to be seen upon the Crea-
> tures . . . so there are also Numberless Lessons of *Morality*,
> which by the Help of the *Analogy* between the *Natural* and
> *Spiritual* World . . . we may learn from them. . . . Truly we
> have a world of *Teachers* about us.

It is a kind of alchemy to "turn the meanest Objects whatso-
ever, into what is far *better than Gold*."

Sitting by a fireside with some friends one cold Massachusetts
day, Mather suggested that they take up this discipline. He boasted

that from the fire burning before them he could fill an entire book with meditations. Taking his own advice, he produced a book of forty meditations on everything from the dancing flames to the tongs for moving logs: "I am going to Discourse *with* and *on* my *Fire*; and fetch from it many *Lessons* of no little Importance." He summarizes the method as a triangular journey: First, go out to the object to make observations. Second, go to the Bible and draw an analogy to its teachings, whether on God's gifts or our duties or our temptations. Third, go to God in prayer for help in living by this biblical advice.

A few examples give a sense of what he means: The nimbleness of the flames reminds him to be swift about his duties, especially preparing for heaven; also flames rise up, and so should his spontaneous prayers throughout the day. A fire will burn low, and as the saying goes, "if the Fire be *not mended*, it will soon be *ended*"; so Mather also needs to "mend," or "amend," his life (which leads to a reminder to take time for self-examination, using the Ten Commandments as a guide). As a fire can be smothered if the wood is piled too closely, so grief and sorrow can smother us if we do not find someone with whom to talk about it. And as tongs can pull out a burning log, so we should rescue others facing spiritual danger. Very occasionally, he changes his writing voice and writes directly to God, but the meditative task is always prayerful, and it seems Mather could say with the fictional John Ames, "You feel that you are with someone."

Both forms of meditation mentioned in Mather's book can still be practiced today, and both will be more fruitful if we do them in writing. The simple process of exploring a text of Scripture and pondering how it applies to our spiritual life may be familiar. Looking at material things and finding metaphors and analogies is probably more of a stretch. It is worth trying though, as an exercise. A walk in the woods or along the shore might be a better starting point than watching a fire. Whatever the subject, considering how God has ordered the natural world can lead us to Scripture, where God's ways are described more clearly. From there it should be a short journey to our own lives of faith.

Putting our meditations into writing, whether on a text of Scripture or on the things of creation, will keep us in the process all the way to completion. It will be far less likely that our attention will drift. The page with the written lesson becomes a clear marker on the pilgrimage of discipleship, pointing the direction we need to go.

AUGUSTINE'S *CONFESSIONS*

These Puritan texts are long out of print, and it is harder still to find the actual journals; many were consigned to the flames by their authors. On the other hand, the best role model of this kind of written prayer lived long before the Puritans, and his book can be found in any bookstore: the *Confessions* of St. Augustine (354-430). This North African professor of rhetoric sowed a lot of wild oats before he became a Christian at thirty-two. Shortly after that he became a bishop, so he had some explaining to do. He defended the integrity of his conversion in a spiritual autobiography written directly to God as a prayer. For fifteen centuries, people have eagerly listened in.

Readers often say Augustine could be telling their own stories. Partly that is because he was such a careful observer of his emotional and spiritual experience. His story also feels familiar because he is far and away the most influential thinker in the history of Western Christianity. In part, we experience the faith as we do because of him and because of this text.

Though he never formally taught the practice of written prayer, Augustine's book-length prayer gives examples of all three of the things we've seen the Puritans teaching. He tells his own life story, trying to discern traces of God's hand in his journey toward conversion. He practices self-examination, admitting his sins and temptations. And he meditates on Scripture and the mysteries of living. Pen in hand, he tries to tell God the truth. Perhaps it is no surprise that the Puritans quoted the *Confessions* fairly frequently. Those who want to see solid examples of written meditative prayer can find them here.

Finding the traces of God. The first half of Augustine's *Confessions* tells of his life from infancy through conversion. The new bishop prays through his own history, trying to discover what God did to make him a Christian and a bishop: "But when shall I be capable of proclaiming by 'the tongue of my pen' (Ps. 44:2) all your exhortations and all your terrors and consolations and directives, by which you brought me to preach your word and dispense your sacrament to your people?" Confessing, telling the truth, requires him to figure out what God was doing all along the way, so he tells God his story. God knows it already, but Augustine is eager to know God better by figuring out what God was doing throughout his life.

On the surface, Augustine is telling the story of his conversion. From early faith, he travelled down through the sins of youth and straight into an addiction to his own lust. He began to find his way to adult faith, but he was stuck. Christ called him to purity; Augustine really liked sex. He famously prayed, "Grant me chastity and continence, but not yet." Finally, God took action and converted him. Augustine was dithering in a garden, unable to choose to follow Christ, weeping with frustration. Then he heard a child's voice from somewhere, saying, "Take and read!" He opened the book beside him, apparently Paul's epistles, at random, and struck on Romans 13:13-14: "Not in reveling and drunkenness, not in debauchery and licentiousness, not in quarreling and jealousy. Instead, put on the Lord Jesus Christ, and make no provision for the flesh, to gratify its desires." It is the least appealing conversion text on record, but it was exactly what he needed. "With your word you pierced my heart and I loved you."

Beneath the basic conversion story is a deep search for the traces of God's actions behind the scenes. Right in the midst of Augustine's sins and struggles, God was there in the details, nudging him toward Christ. I suspect the fact that he was writing helped him slow down enough to find these things; had he just prayed silently about his past he may never have noticed. In retrospect, he saw God working through secular philosophy when, at eighteen, he discovered the book *Hortensius* by Cicero and was convinced to seek wisdom. Though Cicero could not make him a Christian, "It altered my prayers, Lord, to be towards you yourself."

God was also working through Augustine's mixed motives: he took a new job in Rome for selfish reasons, but God used this to get him away from bad company. At the same time, God even used Augustine's sins: he lied to his mother to get away, but it brought him closer to baptism. He knew God was working through his mother, Monica, who prayed for him. She was far away, across miles and oceans, "but you are present everywhere. Where she was, you heard her, and where I was, you had mercy on me."

He thinks hard about those prayers. Sometimes God did not do what she asked, but Augustine still found God working. She prayed that Augustine would stay in Africa, but ultimately her prayer was for his conversion. So "in your deep counsel you heard the central point of her longing." Underneath the apparent "no" was God's resounding "yes!"

When we are living life, it is hard to spot God's hand at work. If we slow down and prayerfully write about our lives, like Augustine we may see it after the fact. No matter how far we may have wandered, most of us also find that God was always there, working in and around us. Life in Christ really is a gift, and the Giver has left a thousand traces for those who have eyes to see.

Telling God the truth. From its title, *Confessions* sounds like it's going to be a list of Augustine's sins. He does a great deal of self-examination, but he is not filled with guilt; he has long known forgiveness. The title actually indicates his intention to tell the truth, and he "confesses" all kinds of things, including God's goodness. His main subject, though, is himself. He has to figure out what the truth about Augustine is before he can tell it. He calls himself "a vast problem" and sometimes asks, "What then am I, my God?" He wants the deep truth, not specific sins but his heart, his motives and desires. Understanding himself will help him know and praise the God who loved him and sought him despite it all.

So, what does he find? Of course he does not remember his infancy, but he extrapolates from babies he has seen. Babies are demanding, and he knows he must have been that way too:

> When I did not get my way, either because I was not understood or lest it be harmful to me, I used to be indignant with my seniors for their disobedience, and with free people who were not slaves to my interests; and I would revenge myself upon them by weeping.

That may not strike us as sinful, but Augustine was looking for the roots of an adult problem: people seek their own interests without concern for others.

His youth he does remember. He tells of stealing someone's pears with a gang of friends just for the fun of it: "If any of those pears entered my mouth, my criminality was the piquant sauce." Recalling and writing about such scenes, he works for a deeper understanding of just what sin really is. Sin was aiming too low. We were created to seek God, to love God above all things. Sin is choosing to love something in creation more than the Creator. In the case of the stolen pears, Augustine chose the small earthly joy of his friends' approval: "These inferior goods have their delights, but not comparable to my God who made them all. It is in him that the just person takes delight; he is the joy of those who are true of heart (Ps. 63:11)."

With this insight in place, Augustine turns to examine his present life prayerfully. He is a leader in a high church office. He is called to love God above all, but he finds that he longs to be praised by people. Therein lies a key temptation for the bishop. Biblical passages on pride and ambition strike home. To lead, he needs to be feared and loved, but that is dangerous, because it is so satisfying. "We cease to find our joy in your truth and place it in the deceitfulness of men. It becomes our pleasure to be loved and feared not for your sake, but instead of you." It is a temptation created for Augustine by the combination of God's genuine calling and his own weaknesses. He has to find a way to live faithfully in the midst of it.

That kind of honesty about his particular temptations is a challenge to me. It is too easy to define sin as disobedience to a rule: don't kill, don't steal, don't commit adultery. We check them off one by one, but obeying the rules pales in comparison to the joy and freedom of loving God personally, above all things. Prayerful self-examination, particularly following Augustine's model of doing it in writing, can refocus our lives on loving God. Though it is countercultural, this, like the "searching and fearless moral inventory" of twelve-step programs, is the path toward growth. When we are honest, there is a place for God's grace to land. If praying in a journal can help us know who we are right now, we can spend our energy on becoming the people God calls us to be.

Meditating on Scripture and creation. The *Confessions* also show Augustine as someone who meditates on Scripture and the mysteries of life, though never in such stylized forms as we saw with Mather. He clearly spent years steeped in Scripture: his prayer is frequently made up of strings of quotations from the Bible, especially the Psalms. He also spends whole chapters praying through a specific passage of Scripture: the creation in Genesis. This is another excellent example of what we can do in prayerful writing. Putting our Bible study into writing in a journal can clarify our thinking and make our encounters with the Bible more prayerful.

Augustine also fills many pages with his meditations on other mysterious things, growing in theological understanding in the process. Sin is one of those mysteries. Another is how memory works; how is it that we can remember that we have forgotten something? In other sections, he ponders the nature of time, music and matter. It is a different form of meditation on creation than Mather taught, but he prays about it all, and it bears fruit because he does it slowly, in writing. It helps him better understand God, as well as how he knows God. That leads him to love and praise God more fully.

We, too, can take some time and write about the mysteries and paradoxes of life in the world God has created. Of course, it is much easier not to dwell on things we do not understand. But if we face what unsettles us and pray through it all the way to the end, we may find ourselves better lovers of God. We might even find ourselves better theologians.

IN the tenth place, when you have read over your Journall, . . . ask your owne hearts these three questions: . . . What honor do I bring to God for all this? . . . What good do I to my neighbour? . . . Ask your own hearts often what good you your selves get by all that God hath done for you.

THE JOURNAL OR DIARY OF A THANKFUL CHRISTIAN

CONCLUSION

If you started out stumped, not knowing what to write about even if you wanted to pray in a journal, you might now find yourself with the opposite problem: the Puritans have assigned way too many tasks. The idea, though, is not to do all of these things. I hope, instead, that you have found just one that sounds interesting, useful, even fun. Give it a try.

If you are not sure, take the various tasks in turn, and do them over a period of time. Write out your reflections on God's actions in your past and present life, recording your gratitude. Examine your life and write about the state of your soul, writing to God about how to move forward on the road toward spiritual maturity. Write out your meditations and reflections, whether on a passage of Scripture or on something in the world that seems to point you toward God. Even if you do not find journaling is something you want to continue all the time, you may have added a skill and a resource to your prayer life for some time in the future when you really need it.

PRAYING WITH
THE CLOUD OF UNKNOWING

Contemplation in the Dark

Lift up your heart to God with a humble impulse of love; and have him as your aim, not any of his goods. Take care that you avoid thinking of anything but himself, so that there is nothing for your reason or your will to work on, except himself. Do all that in you lies to forget all the creatures that God ever made, and their works, so that neither your thought nor your desire be directed or extended to any of them, neither in general nor in particular. Let them alone and pay no attention to them.

THE CLOUD OF UNKNOWING

The method of prayer taught in the anonymous medieval book *The Cloud of Unknowing* is simple: focus your attention on God. That's it.

Did it go by too quickly? Here it comes again: Turn directly toward God—turn your mind, your will, your soul—in an outpouring of love. Then keep your focus there, every moment, day after day, always. According to the author, when you do that you see nothing, feel nothing and really know nothing. It is like climbing a mountain, way up into the fog, and losing your bearings. Rather than sensing the presence of God, in prayer we enter a "cloud of unknowing" and stay there. As with many "simple" things, it is exceptionally difficult to do.

When people hear they are to pray without senses or emotions or words or ideas, they often have trouble figuring out what they actually *are* supposed to do. Imagining this as their prayer life for the rest of their days can be daunting. Then when they try it out, the typical response is, "I just don't see how doing this is actually prayer." Meditation perhaps, but prayer? With no requests, no conversation—no words of any kind?

CONTEMPLATIVE PRAYER

This is indeed prayer—contemplative prayer. Contemplation, by definition, is about looking at something. Contemplative prayer directs our gaze toward God. It fits the ancient definition of prayer as communion better than today's common view that prayer is conversation. Actually, with this form of contemplative prayer we approach the territory of mysticism. *The Cloud of Unknowing* aims for a direct, unmediated encounter with God, which exactly fits the definition of the mystical element of Christianity offered by Bernard McGinn in his monumental history of Western mysticism.

This method of prayer, and this direct encounter with God, are hard to describe because all the words we use are laden with metaphors that point to creation rather than to the Creator. You could say *The Cloud of Unknowing* has you "look" toward God, but that implies something visual. The author is adamant that we do not see; our eyes can see only the creation. We could say we turn our "hearts" toward God, but that sounds sensory, emotional. Feelings also are part of creation, something less than a direct encounter with God. Say that we turn our "minds" toward God, and it sounds like thinking, which requires earthly words and concepts. We aim to encounter the living God, not our ideas about God.

Personally, I find the *Cloud*'s approach extremely comforting. I do not think I am alone in feeling inferior when people start to talk about their marvelous experiences in prayer: they sensed God's presence or heard God's voice or were overcome by feelings of love. The rest of us cringe and think, *I guess I really am no good at prayer after all.* We have done our time, showing up at prayer for years or decades, and felt nothing. Where was God? Why do we never get any of the goodies? To all who pray and feel absolutely nothing, *The Cloud of Unknowing* says, "That is good. That is the sign that you really are in the presence of God." We know God is there *because* we feel nothing. If we feel some*thing* we can know for sure that it is something in creation—not the direct, unmediated presence of God.

Beyond being a validation of many people's experience of prayer, *The Cloud of Unknowing* can blow the socks off Christians raised in other approaches. I knew one loving and faithful man who had been raised in an evangelical home. In his world, they did not talk about contemplation. They focused on intercession and supplication, even if they described it as conversation with God. Praying better meant praying longer and asking harder. To him, asking God to do things felt cold and empty; he assumed he was just not a prayer guy. When he read the *Cloud* he exclaimed, "I never realized prayer could mean just *being* with God!" When he spent time directing his loving attention directly toward God, prayer became life giving.

Many ordinary modern people are actually contemplatives at heart, whether they like the term or not. Many others face circumstances in which standing silent before the majesty of God is far better than speaking. The *Cloud* provides a way for them to pray.

LAYERS OF MYSTERY

There are layers of mystery around *The Cloud of Unknowing*. First, it was written anonymously in fourteenth-century England. Scholars deduce that the writer was probably a Carthusian monk, perhaps a priest, and the anonymity probably expresses the author's humility. Second, he writes in a tradition within Christian spiritual theology that grows from another mysterious, anonymous author. Back in the sixth century, someone in the Greek-speaking world wrote a series of books as if he were Dionysius the Areopagite, a convert of Paul's ministry (Acts 17:34). In the ancient world, writing under an assumed name was not uncommon. It could preserve humility for the author and borrow credibility for the writings: if they were written by someone taught by Paul, they would be next door to Scripture.

Dionysius' works, including an important one called "Mystical Theology," have been very influential in the history of Christian spirituality, both East and West. These days the writer is known as "pseudo-Dionysius" or "Dionysius the pseudo-Areopagite," because it has been clear for centuries that these texts are informed by much later Christian writings. Just who wrote them remains a mystery.

A third layer of mystery is the actual teaching of both authors, since at one point the author of the *Cloud* says that there is nothing in his book that is not found in Dionysius. God is very, very mysterious. That awareness of the mysteriousness of God is not the same thing as mysticism. The word *mysticism* puts many Christians on their guard. Many assume that mysticism is inherently non-Christian, a characteristic only of Eastern religions. However, historians of Christianity have to acknowledge that many of the most significant theologians, East and West, have written positively on the topic.

There has always been a mystical element in Christianity, and according to McGinn, it includes not only the direct encounter with God, but also things people do to prepare for it and the ways life is changed as a result of it. I find it ironic that it is often Reformed and evangelical writers who are most opposed to mysticism. Calvin often treated the Christian faith as "union with Christ," and evangelicals almost invariably call it "a personal relationship" with God or Christ. Both descriptions express brilliantly the idea of an unmediated encounter with God. So it seems like mystics who do not know they are mystics are being critical of mystics who do.

For the Dionysian tradition, though, the sheer mystery of God is crucial, and for the *Cloud* author this has enormous implications for prayer. This tradition is deeply influenced by neo-Platonic philosophy, as was the great majority of Christian theology from the third through the twelfth centuries. It understands that there is a vast distance, a categorical difference, between God and created human beings. I compare it to the difference between the two-dimensional world of a cartoon and the three-dimensional existence of the artist who draws it. If the cartoon characters came to life on the page, they might hear about their artist who lives in a mysterious third dimension of "depth." But they would be incapable of stepping off the page to experience depth. They could never wrap their paper-flat imaginations around it, even if they cried out in little speech bubbles, "O artist, I believe in you! Help me understand your 'depth'!" Any attempt at drawing in 3-D for them would just be an illusion.

Similarly for us, stuck in our world, we can't really grasp the timeless eternity of the God who invented time, except in terms of time going on and on. And we can only imagine God existing in a place even though God created the very space of our universe. Our thinking is limited by the categories of the created world, and so we can't ever grasp God as God is. (And notice the metaphor inherent in the word *grasp*: it implies that what we grasp must be small enough to be surrounded by our hand. God is bigger than that—even if the concept of size is irrelevant.)

Of course, each of us can speak as personally and truly as Paul, saying, "I know the one in whom I have put my trust" (2 Timothy 1:12). However, it is easy to claim too much, as if we have absolute and complete knowledge about God. Pseudo-Dionysius and the *Cloud* author would have us think hard about how we know God.

We may start with our senses, looking at a star-filled sky, and think, "Wow! I see the glory of God!" Do we really? We see God's handiwork. It shines with the reflection of God's grandeur, but it is a reflection. Then maybe we look inside, remembering a life-changing spiritual experience when we were overwhelmed with God's love. "I felt it!" we say, "That was God." Or was it? We felt the effect of God's action, like the wake behind a boat—but the boat has passed. The feeling was within the capacity of our senses and emotions, still nowhere near God's essence. So we turn to words—perhaps the words of Scripture. God's Word reliably teaches us who God is. But even a Word-centered theologian like John Calvin would tell you that Scripture reveals to us what God chooses to reveal. Get a thorough grasp of the Bible's teaching and we will know what we need for salvation. But there is more to God than that. God is far greater than anything we can say about him. Our minds can know all of this. Maybe then our minds can bring true knowledge of God. Certainly our minds can grasp more than we can put into words, but

> *The work consists in treading down of the awareness of all the creatures that God ever made, and in keeping them under the cloud of forgetting, as we mentioned before. Here is all the labour; for this, with the help of grace, is man's work. And the other beyond this, the impulse of love, this is the work of God alone. So press on with your own work, and he, I promise you, will certainly not fail in his.*
>
> THE CLOUD OF UNKNOWING

even the best thoughts of the best theologian are merely thoughts about God. God himself remains beyond our grasp—a mystery.

The Cloud of Unknowing brings this into the practical realm of prayer. The author's method of pushing the conscious attention of prayer toward God and dwelling there in his presence makes sense in a way, but it is paradoxical. Being in God's presence, he tells us, leads to "unknowing" rather than "knowing." We see nothing, feel nothing, know nothing. If we were in a cloud, floating in a fog, we would know nothing in any ordinary way, not even what is up or down, because on every side would be gray.

Paradoxes are hard to manage. Even if people can see it as prayer, when they try to do what the *Cloud* author says problems and questions arise. The questions fall into patterns, and many of them are the very topics addressed in the book. Perhaps that is why in the preface he pleads with readers to read all to the way to the end: he knows he is going to answer most of their question. If he were a website manager rather than a medieval monk, I suspect he would have put much of this in a section of Frequently Asked Questions. I decided to do that for him.

THEOLOGY

Question: Is this actually even Christian? I mean, God has made himself known in Jesus Christ, but this asks me to meditate on an unknowable God. You can't build solid doctrine from that.

Answer: It is genuinely Christian. To see that, perhaps the best starting place is to read *The Life of Moses* by Gregory of Nyssa. Gregory was one of the three great Cappadocian theologians of the fourth century who almost define what orthodoxy is. He portrays our spiritual journey using Moses' experiences as a metaphor: when Moses went up to meet God face to face, he entered a dark cloud and stayed in it for forty days. Hearing some of these concepts from someone whose credentials are unquestionable can make room for us to hear them from a text like the *Cloud*.

Beyond that, it is important to remember that historically Christians have done more than one kind of theological work. In particular, in addition to doctrinal theology, there is spiritual theology. The sound spiritual theologian starts with good doctrine firmly in place, but asks different questions—like how a finite, sinful, created person can enter into prayerful communion with the infinite, holy Creator God.

The *Cloud* was written back when there was an active Inquisition, and if it contained heretical doctrine, it would likely not have come down through history unquestioned. It is not typical of Protestant theology, Reformed theology or evangelical theology, but it is not at all outside the scope of Christian theology.

TIME, METHODS, DIRECTIONS

Question: I want to try this out but am not sure how to start. Does this kind of prayer take a long time? I mean, can I do it in my daily quiet time?

Answer: As with many things in this approach, the answer is a little paradoxical. It does not take any time at all; it also takes the rest of your life. The act of turning your attention directly to God happens in an instant, and that action is prayer. On the other hand, you have to keep doing it, instant after instant. The author recommends beginning with a regular time for prayer. When I teach this, I have people start with just five minutes a day, and that is often more than people can handle. Determining whether it is a good approach for you personally will take some time. You have to get familiar enough with it that you are not squirming out of your skin or bored to pieces, and then spend a bit more time to see how it goes.

Question: But how can I "think" about God if Dionysian spiritual theology teaches that God is bigger than my mind's capacity? I can think about what God *does*, but I can't wrap my mind around what God *is*. Is this another paradox?

Answer: Actually, no. *Think* is the wrong word. The attention you should aim toward God is loving. Thinking and loving are very different kinds of abilities. The *Cloud* puts it like this: "But no man can think of God himself. . . . He can certainly be loved, but not thought." The author frequently summarizes the basic method, and love is the most frequent description. To cite just one example, "With a devout, pleasing, impulsive love strive to pierce that darkness above you. You are to smite upon that thick cloud of unknowing with a sharp dart of longing love." God is beyond our minds' grasp, but with love we can hold on tight.

Question: So if God is like a cloud above me, am I supposed to look up toward the sky? If I'm inside, am I supposed to stare at the ceiling?

Answer: Basically, no. All the descriptions are laden with metaphors, and he goes to enormous lengths to keep readers from taking spiritual metaphors in a literal, physical way. Although the Bible sometimes portrays heaven as "up," even in the fourteenth century theologians knew that God is just as close if you look down, left or right, or inside yourself: "For in the spiritual realm, height and depth, length and breadth, are all the same." The distance to heaven, he says, is measured in desire, not in yards. God is all around us. If we have a pure desire for the presence of God, that loving attention is heaven. The author does say that if the Spirit prompts you to lift your hands or look upward, you should do so. Otherwise, and generally, this would be misguided. We should not be striving physically to see or to move our hearts. People who do that just get exhausted and are prey to visions sent by the devil to delude them.

Question: Isn't this basically the same as what we read in Brother Lawrence's *The Practice of the Presence of God*?

Answer: The two are vastly different. Brother Lawrence has clear concepts of God in mind, and his way of prayer is constant verbal conversation. The *Cloud* turns away from concepts and sits in silence in God's presence.

HELPS AND DISTRACTIONS

Question: How am I supposed to quiet my mind so that I can give God my full attention?

Answer: Actually, the process is exactly the opposite. You can't quiet your mind first. You turn your attention toward God, and then as any kind of thought creeps in, you gently set it aside, under the "cloud of forgetting."

Question: When I pray or meditate, I find it helps to have a candle or a holy icon before me to help me focus. Is that okay in this method?

Answer: Not if you are a purist. When you pray this way, nothing (no "thing") can be between you and God. Not even the Bible should be between us and God, though the *Cloud*'s author does recommend meditation on the Bible in other contexts.

Let me explain. The author portrays this kind of prayer using a spatial metaphor: You are in the middle with "clouds" both above and below—not unlike looking out of an airplane window on a rainy day. God alone is "above" you, and all creation is "below" you. The clouds are of two different kinds.

As you push up toward the presence of God, you find the "cloud of unknowing." This describes the very nature of the situation: it indicates your lack of ability to know God. It will always be there because the God you are contemplating is always

As long as a man lives in this mortal flesh, he will always see and feel this thick cloud of unknowing between himself and God. And not only that, but it is one of the painful results of original sin that he will always see and feel that some of the many creatures that God made, or some of their works, will always be inserting themselves in his awareness, between himself and God.

THE CLOUD OF UNKNOWING

beyond your understanding. You are in direct contact with God, but God is beyond words or concepts.

On the other hand, the cloud below is there because you put it there. He wants you to bring a "cloud of forgetting" between yourself and all of creation. Since you are putting your attention directly on God, you must take your attention off absolutely everything that is not God. You must choose to "forget" it. It is not that you develop permanent amnesia. Rather, while you pray, you set every thing aside.

Keeping this metaphor in mind helps make sense of this way of praying. If you are trying to gaze up toward God, but your attention is even partly on something in creation, then you are putting that thing "above" you, between you and God. I think the author of *The Cloud of Unknowing* would say that looking at icons while praying would place them between you and God. Of course, the Orthodox place icons between themselves and God on purpose, as windows through which their attention goes to God, but that is another story.

Question: Sometimes when I'm really quiet in prayer, it seems like God is speaking to me. Or prayer can bring the peace of mind I need, and important insights come to me. Should I stop and write these things down or something?

Answer: The author would say no, not in a time devoted to this kind of prayer. The purpose of this time of prayer is to be in God's presence, and even an excellent and useful insight is less than God. No thing can be allowed to take your attention away from God—it can't be above you, between you and God—and even a thought is a "thing," part of this created world. You are already setting aside countless tasks and obligations to have time for prayer. Setting aside good thoughts is necessary as well. Trust that if you really need that insight, God will bring it back after prayer.

Question: My problem is not insight but distraction. When I try to sit still and focus on God the way the *Cloud* says to, my own thoughts always start to creep back in. Any practical advice?

Answer: The author acknowledges that this happens all the time. He has helpful ideas, though he says you will probably learn better tricks and tools for dealing with distracting thoughts through your own experience.

One suggestion is not to wrench your thoughts violently back to God or to deny the thoughts. Instead, enter into dialogue with them. Tell them you know they are there, but now is not the time. Then you can gently set them aside and return your attention to God.

Another approach is to imagine the thoughts in an almost physical way. As the distracting thought approaches, look over its shoulder and push your way around it to give your attention to God. You can picture a running back in a football game pushing off of the opposing player's shoulder to avoid a tackle and move toward the goal line.

Finally, he suggests admitting defeat: "Cower down under them like a poor wretch and a coward overcome in battle." This is really an attempt to give yourself over to the care of God, who can be trusted to come to your help.

Question: My problem is boredom and confusion. I need some help in keeping my attention on God moment by moment. Am I stuck?

Answer: Our minds use words to direct our thoughts. The author suggests you use a word to draw your attention back to God, slowly repeating it inside your mind as you pray. I suspect that if pressed, he would say that even a word can be "above" us and therefore "between" us and God, but he offers three examples of words he thinks are helpful.

The most important is *God*. God is, after all, the one we are praying to. Saying "God" is a helpful reminder to return our fundamentally wordless attention to God. Second, he suggests we repeat the word *love*. Since love is the faculty we are trying to direct toward God, this also is a helpful way to refocus.

Third, he suggests that sometimes we should say *sin*. He does not want us to think about particular sins. This word is to prompt a sort of inward general confession, reminding us that our whole life is a "congealed lump" of sin. He does not want us to get puffed up about our contemplative practice, so saying "sin" brings us back to honesty and repentance. Slow and gentle repetition of an appropriate word can be a tool to bring our focus back.

MEDITATION? MANTRAS?

Question: This does not really seem like prayer to me. This seems more like meditation.

Answer: Actually, it is quite different from what people in the Middle Ages called meditation. Back then, meditation was an active mental activity. Typically, one would take a verse of Scripture and ruminate on it like a cow chewing its cud. What the *Cloud* teaches is similar to more modern definitions of meditation. Two prominent approaches to meditation ("Centering Prayer" and "Christian Meditation") draw on the *Cloud*. If you find it helpful to practice it as a form of meditation, I think that is fine. I suspect you will discover that you actually are praying.

Question: To me this sounds a lot like meditation in Eastern religions. I've heard they also use "mantras" or repeated phrases and focus on emptying the mind.

Answer: John Main, a monk and priest who taught what he called "Christian Meditation," saw strong similarities between Hindu meditation and *The Cloud of Unknowing*. He was not inclined to emphasize the differences, and this has led to criticism. He learned meditation from a Hindu teacher before learning of Christian sources like the *Cloud*, and that makes some suspicious. I am not convinced that he interpreted the *Cloud* accurately.

The chief similarity is repetition of a word. The differences are stronger. While some Eastern forms of meditation teach people to repeat words they do not understand, the *Cloud* does not suggest just any word, and certainly not a meaningless word. As discussed above, the author favors *God*, *love* or *sin*, and it is the meaning of these words that helps us return our attention to God.

This points to a second radical difference between the *Cloud* and at least the stereotypical Western understanding of meditation in Eastern religions. This is not an exercise in relaxation or an attempt to empty the mind. This way of prayer intends to fill the mind, but to fill it with attention to God. Rational thoughts, images in the imagination and feelings are all set aside because they are simply not God. That is the paradox: a mind focused on God is full of what the mind is not able to grasp; the process is "unknowing" instead of rational "knowing."

FEELINGS

Question: What will I see or feel when I first turn my attention toward God in prayer?

Answer: Nothing.

Question: Is it my fault that I feel nothing when I pray?

Answer: Actually, there is no "fault" in this. It is the nature of being a finite creature trying to be in communion with an infinite God.

Question: Once I get good at it, can I expect to have some sense of God's presence?

Answer: No. You should expect to always feel absolutely nothing. The author does note that God lets some people feel "consolations" in prayer, but he also notes that any such gift is up to God. He also says people making progress in this way of praying have a sense of satisfaction with it. Progress, though, does not indicate personal virtue. He observes that sometimes the people whose lives have been the most clearly sinful make the quickest progress. For this, he draws on the Gospel story of the woman who bathed Jesus' feet with her tears, loving much because she had been forgiven much.

Question: But you said that this loving desire for God "is heaven." If when I pray this way I'm in heaven, then shouldn't it feel good?

Answer: Feelings are irrelevant, variable and unreliable. The author quips that this love or desire for God is heaven because it is the direct, unmediated presence of God. If our God is a consuming, purifying fire, God's presence may feel far from heavenly.

Some people get lovely experiences from praying this way, and others do not. Some people work very hard for a very long time before there is a sense of progress, and some people seem to get it right away. Different people's experiences are different as they encounter the same living God. The author cautions readers never to judge another person's experience based on their own. Even if you do have some "consolations," it is crucial to remember that these are not God. No matter what you experience, there is a cloud of unknowing between you and God.

> |||||||||||||||||||||||||||||||||||||||||||||||||||||||||||||||
>
> *If, then, you are determined to stand and not to fall, never cease from your endeavour, but constantly beat with a sharp dart of longing love upon this cloud of unknowing which is between you and your God. Avoid thinking of anything under God and do not leave this exercise no matter what happens. For it alone, of itself, destroys the root and the ground of sin.*
>
> THE CLOUD OF UNKNOWING
>
> |||||||||||||||||||||||||||||||||||||||||||||||||||||||||||||||

CONTEMPLATIVE LIFE

Question: How am I supposed to spend all my time just focusing on God? I have a job and a family to take care of.

Answer: The author does not think that this method is for everyone, and you have to decide for yourself whether to do it. As was typical in the Middle Ages, he divides all Christians into two groups: the "actives" and the "contemplatives." Both were to live as Christians, but their callings were different. Typically, actives were busy working in the world, whether as laypeople or as priests. Contemplatives could pursue their calling in monastic communities.

The author divides both kinds of life into "higher" and "lower" parts, and they overlap: the higher portion of active life is really the same as the lower part of contemplative life. That means he actually describes three kinds of Christian living.

The lower active life is actions of love: good and holy things done in the world. Above this come spiritual practices like meditation on Scripture: prayerful and studious disciplines that engage your mind and imagination. These make up both the higher part of active life and the lower part of contemplative life. The third level is the height of contemplation, when one moves beyond thinking to loving God directly, pushing upward into the cloud of unknowing and forgetting all created things.

This way of prayer is really for those called to the contemplative life. Protestants often only approve of an active life, or at least we do not create many structures for people to pursue contemplation or any other kind of prayer as a life calling. The *Cloud* author might disagree, but I think many Protestant people are capable of practicing this kind of contemplation even in the midst of "active" life. It would not be something done constantly, sitting alone in stillness. It would be a frequent return of the loving heart between and during activities.

Question: Isn't this "contemplative life" kind of a selfish way of living? I mean, shouldn't I be praying for the needs of the world? Aren't our efforts needed to do Christ's work in the world? I would feel guilty doing this.

Answer: If you find yourself drawn to this kind of prayer, which really is not directly about asking God to help people, and if you feel drawn to it as a way of life, it may indeed preclude some kinds of outward service. That is hard for people committed to the active life to accept. When the Protestant churches broke away from the Catholic Church in the 1500s, it was common to complain that all monks and nuns were selfishly running away from the world when they should be living lives of loving service. Many still hold this attitude. That is unfortunate, because it places a limit on what God might call people to do.

You can see, then, that we must focus all our attention on this meek stirring of love in our will. And with regard to all other sweetnesses and consolations, sensible or spiritual, no matter how pleasing they are, no matter how holy, we should have a sort of heedlessness, if this can be said without failing in courtesy and seemliness. . . . For when love is chaste and perfect . . . it is well satisfied to do without them, if such be God's will.

THE CLOUD OF UNKNOWING

When Jesus was asked about the most important command, he answered that it is to "love the Lord your God with all your heart, and with all your soul, and with all your mind, and with all your strength" (Mark 12:30), and close on its heels is to love your neighbor as yourself. Holiness is to give God first place in all things, to love God above all things. The *Cloud* author argues that this method of prayer is the most direct embodiment of that first and greatest command. When we practice it, we are, in essence, focusing entirely on loving God above all. He would say that this is the best service you can actually do for your neighbor.

Personally, I think it is ironic that anyone who says they want to love God with everything holds back from a kind of prayer that is all about giving God our full attention. Augustine would say that if we do love God above all, our loves for all other things fall into proper proportion. That will include loving our neighbor as ourself.

But there are different ways of serving others. One is to serve the community as a whole by offering more of the prayer that we all owe God. I would add that if you are really directing your love to God in prayer, he will be reshaping your life so that you have some actual love to give to your neighbor. Contemplation is no excuse for selfishness, and you can measure the reality of an encounter with God by whether it produces love of neighbor.

Question: Even if Christians in the past made more room for a calling to contemplative life, is it biblical?

Answer: The author bases his view squarely on Scripture, in a traditionally Catholic way. He uses the biblical story of Mary and Martha. Martha, you will remember, did all the work of cooking and serving, while Mary sat at Jesus' feet and listened. For this author, and for most in the Middle Ages, these women symbolized the active and the contemplative life. In the story, Jesus said that Mary had chosen the best way, and that made a life of holy contemplation legitimate. You may or may not agree that it justifies prayer as a life calling, but it does show that Jesus approves of spending time sitting quietly in his presence.

Question: I thought that Teresa of Ávila said that contemplation is something given as a gift by God. How come *The Cloud of Unknowing* makes it an activity that we can choose?

Answer: Teresa of Ávila describes the highest level of union with God as "infused contemplation." This is something that comes as pure gift, not something we can do. She also describes lots of things that we can do in prayer that are described as contemplation—acquired contemplation. The *Cloud* author, on the other hand, is describing a different kind of contemplative prayer than Teresa. Here the basic action of contemplation is within our ability. However, just as in Teresa's infused contemplation, here too there is divine initiative: this form of prayer is for those whom God calls. If God is calling you to it, he can be expected to give you the capacity for it.

PARADOX AND CALLING

Question: I still don't feel like I'm praying. I'm not actually doing anything.

Answer: Yes, since your senses, mind and imagination are not useful in grasping the God you are focused on, you often seem to be doing nothing when you pray this way. If you are doing it right, the author tells us, perhaps with a wink, you are also "nowhere" while you do nothing. That is, if your attention is directly on God, with all of creation pressed down below the "cloud of forgetting," it is not about being in any particular place.

Question: It still sounds pretty weird to me. Do I have to do it?

Answer: Not unless you are in my prayer class—then you have to do it for two weeks. More seriously, though, the author is quite clear that this is not for everyone. He tells us that we should listen closely to our reactions to what we read or hear about this way of prayer. If it does not even sound appealing, it is very unlikely that it is your calling. No problem there: you are definitely called to pray, and there are lots of other ways to pray. But be sure you understand it before you reject it. Someday you may meet someone for whom this would be an ideal way to pray.

On the other hand, if this does draw you, perhaps in a way you can't even explain, then this wordless, imageless, nonintellectual way of communion with God may be for you. The calling to contemplative prayer is a gift of grace. It can be full of blessing—as you might expect if it really is contact with God. Still, you should not expect tangible, material or emotional rewards.

If you do have good feelings as a result of prayer, don't worry. If you keep at it, you will surely get past them and into the presence of God.

PART FOUR

ASKING GOD FOR HELP

Is there anyone among you who, if your child asks for bread, will give a
stone? Or if the child asks for a fish, will give a snake? If you then, who
are evil, know how to give good gifts to your children, how much more
will your Father in heaven give good things to those who ask him!

MATTHEW 7:9-11

For many people, prayer is fundamentally about making requests
of God: we ask God's help in our own trials and tribulations, for
family and friends, for the work of the church, for peace. Jesus was
maybe a little too frank in calling his disciples "evil" when he told
them that their Father in heaven would give them good things in
response to their prayers. But he speaks good news: he promises
that God not only hears but also answers. No matter how generous and loving we are as parents, God is even better.

The two approaches in this section are influential examples of
taking seriously Jesus' invitation to ask God for help. I put it last on
purpose, because if we start with prayer as asking for things, we
risk nurturing a lopsided relationship with God. If we think God is

obliged to grant our every request, we are misguided. It is more important that we are God's servants, doing what God asks of us. Then we can be grateful that God invites and expects our requests.

The ways of praying from earlier sections nurture a healthy spiritual life, drawing us close to God, filling us with love and reverence. I hope that readers take up at least one of them. That will make us more likely to ask for the kinds of things God wants to give. Then in confident faith, we, God's beloved children, will ask what we really need. Agnes Sanford and Andrew Murray made intercessory prayer their ministry, and in very different ways. They provide wise guidance to us as we, too, bring our concerns to God. Whether it is the heart of our vocation or not, we all need ways to ask God's help.

9

PRAYING WITH AGNES SANFORD

The Healing Light

When we ask for the indwelling of God's Holy Spirit in the body, let us think of that part of the body that most needs His life. Let us imagine His light and life glowing there like a fire, shining like a light. Then through the rest of the day let us continually give thanks that His life is at work within us accomplishing His perfect will and recreating us after His image and likeness, which is perfection.

Christ is the healer. No human being has the power to heal. Christ loves all of us, and sends His love through us to His children according to His will. If we quiet ourselves and let Him speak, we will not go wrong.

AGNES SANFORD,
The Healing Light

W̲hen people read *The Healing Light* by Agnes Sanford (1897-1982), usually no one is in the middle. Some love her; some loathe her. She taught about praying for healing—not just for inner peace in the face of illness, but for miraculous cures. Many whose faith is rooted in traditional and rational kinds of theology seem particularly opposed, but it can be personal. As one man said to me, "This kind of thing is offensive. You can't just tell people their prayers aren't answered because they don't have enough faith. I have type 1 diabetes. You think I haven't prayed for God to heal me?"

But there is another side. Many with roots in the charismatic tradition are drawn to Sanford, but there are others—including, in my observation, many with artistic temperaments and some with experience in health professions. One told me, "I felt like Agnes Sanford was putting into words what I have felt about prayer my whole life." Another said, "This reminded me of when my daughter was little. She was sick and I laid my hands on her and prayed. She complained about the 'hot burning feeling' she felt from my hands."

Sanford is also a polarizing figure among those concerned with relevant issues professionally. She is widely credited with (or blamed for) influencing the charismatic practice of Christian healing, and for her emphasis on the "healing of memories." Admirers include Francis McNutt, one of the early Catholic priests in the charismatic movement and the writer of *Healing*—something of a classic on the topic. The team of Dennis and Matthew Linn and Sheila Fabricant, who write on prayer from an Ignatian perspective, dedicated the book *Praying with Another for Healing* to Sanford and McNutt. Evangelical Protestant Leanne Payne quotes Sanford admiringly in *The Healing Presence*. Yet on the other side is the volume *Abusing Memory* by Jane Gumprecht, M.D., which portrays Sanford's theology as dangerous, far more New Age than Christian. Both sides can make solid points.

AGNES SANFORD? REALLY?

Well then, why Agnes Sanford? If she is a recent polarizing figure accused of New Age views, why include her in a book on great teachers from great traditions? Several reasons.

First, Sanford represents the charismatic movement, the mainline flowering of Pentecostalism. These twentieth-century movements have changed the face of global Christianity and after only a century represent a quarter of the world's Christians. It would be irresponsible not to explore some of their distinctive teachings on prayer. Their defining feature is the recovery and use of the New Testament spiritual gifts, including healing. No one knows who among their teachers will stand the test of time, but Sanford was early and influential.

A second reason to include Sanford is that Christians everywhere seem to want to pray for healing. Listen to prayer requests in small groups, worship services or over coffee. The most frequent issue is healing. Someone has cancer, a heart attack, Alzheimer's. Paul may be right that death has lost its sting, but illness is still mighty scary. We urgently pray. We also have doubts and questions, especially if our churches teach that miracles ended with the apostles, or if our scientific minds do not believe God intervenes in a world of natural law.

A third reason is the New Testament. When you see how much of Jesus' ministry focused on healing, it starts to look like it was pretty important to him. When you hear him promise that we will do works just like his and that he will surely answer prayers (John 14:12-13), it can seem strange that we do not see more healing. If someone like Sanford had even a little practical insight about praying for healing, perhaps we should listen to her.

And this is my fourth reason to include Sanford here: even if her theology raises some problems, she testifies to remarkable things. She prayed, and God healed. Most of us would like to experience that. For some people, intercession—especially for healing—is their life calling, and they need tools. However, even if this is not our vocation, Sanford teaches useful lessons.

I hope readers have grown to appreciate the deep theological roots of the approaches to prayer throughout this book; prayer is serious stuff. Sanford did not write academic theology. In fact, she is a tad inconsistent about how many steps there are to prayer for healing and just what goes on in each one. But it is possible to have practical and spiritual wisdom even without theological subtlety. I hope that all will approach her, or any teaching on prayer, with analytical skills intact, ready to sift the wheat from the chaff. There are treasures here, hidden amid obvious problems. Hold fast to what is true, and leave the rest behind. If we can benefit only from teachers whose theology is flawless, we can't learn from anyone.

LEARNING TO PRAY FOR HEALING
I want to spend most of the chapter looking just at the wheat and ignoring the chaff. I will return at the end to some of the problems and dangers, but I want to ensure people see the good things. Sanford is not systematic but she has a distinctive method, though all her lessons need a bit of polishing to ensure that they shine with the wisdom God gave her.

Teachers of intercessory prayer usually emphasize that God's promise to answer requires that we have faith. Sanford's great gift is that her approaches build faith. She teaches practical things that you can do to pray joyfully and confidently rather than in desperation and despair. This is a major virtue. It gets us out of a paradox: Jesus promises to answer if we pray with true faith, but we know our faith is weak. And we cannot manufacture the faith we need, as both Paul and our daily experience agree. So Jesus' promise provides little comfort. Even less comforting is being told by some well-meaning Christian that our heartfelt prayer went unanswered because we did not have enough faith.

Sanford would agree that faith is required, and I think she would agree that faith comes as a gift. She knows, though, that God can give a gift as a seed; it needs to be watered to grow. She teaches us how to tend and nurture faith. Then, with a deep and growing sense of God's goodness and active concern, we can approach God confidently. A growing faith changes us. We can rest in God's care, no matter how God responds to a particular request; we do not need God to give us our way. With a heart full of trust, we can also relax and see where God really does answer.

THE BASIC PROCESS

Sanford's approaches to prayer for healing include both a basic process and specific ways to use the imagination. They are interrelated, but for clarity's sake, I will separate them. Her basic process has four steps—or three plus an attitude adjustment.

Step one: Connect to God, and deepen the connection. Sanford tells us that before asking God to heal, we must begin by drawing close to God. She uses electricity as an analogy (relentlessly), portraying unanswered prayer as a wiring problem. If your toaster doesn't work, you make sure it is plugged in; similarly, we need a good connection to God for healing power to flow. If people can get past the crass comparison of prayer to a household appliance, some still object to the idea that something in us could prevent God from answering prayer. Of course God is free and can do anything. Sanford's point, though, is that if we live far from God as strangers or rebels, asking God to do extraordinary things is presumptuous.

Also, rather than having the confidence of faith, we often come to prayer full of our own anxieties, troubles and strivings. To start the conversation, we need to turn our hearts to God in repentance, to quiet ourselves in reverence. This is not an unusual teaching: many say to start by centering ourselves, becoming aware of God's presence, or to begin with praise and thanksgiving. We need to draw near if we would be heard, and drawing near builds faith.

Sanford has good practical suggestions about this. First, she recommends we pick a daily time to practice prayer. Second, she tells us to relax our bodies and minds, finding a physical position that can be alert and comfortable. She suggests we not slouch, and she does not favor kneeling. Better to sit with good posture. Third, she has us focus our minds on God—not empty our minds, but fill them with God. Finally, she has us call out to God, but not yet to ask for healing. We ask God to be with us and fill us. She prays, "Heavenly Father, please increase in me at this time Your life-giving power," or she simply asks for God the giver of life to be present.

This is Sanford's preparation for prayers that prompt God to answer, but it is not self-serving. As she puts it, "We find after a while that we desire God more for His own sake than for ours." Prayer for healing flows from being in God's presence, because healing reflects the character and will of God.

Step two: Make a specific request, and move to thankfulness. The next step begins with what I can only call Sanford's pseudo-scientific perspective. She envisions prayer as an experimental research project. Now that we have plugged in to God's power, "we must decide on some tangible thing that we wish accomplished by that power, so that we can know without question whether our experiment succeeded or failed." We will learn to pray by asking for something absolutely specific and seeing how God responds.

For many Christians, that is hard. I have spoken to many who humbly hesitate to ever make specific requests of God and who would find it presumptuous to make God the subject of scientific inquiry. We end our prayers "yet not my will, but thine be done," which can express reverent trust that God will do what is best. But as Sanford points out, it can also express a distrust that God can heal, or wants to heal. In practice it can sometimes amount to withdrawing the request we've just made. To Sanford, this fails to make the experiment, and the experiment is what nurtures faith, or trust in God and God's love.

Think about how trust is built in human relationships. If someone asks a favor, we learn that he or she trusts us. Asking help draws people closer together. Sanford urges us to do something similar with God: we build trust in God by making an honest request of him. We watch for an answer to complete the experiment, since seeing God at work in response to our request builds faith, giving us confidence to ask again.

Sanford wants us to be specific, but she tells us to make our request only the first time we pray for something. When we pray about it again, we should focus on giving thanks. This is even more helpful in nurturing faith, because it works against our tendency to confuse prayer with worrying. If we come back to prayer and make the request again—and again, and again—we seem to assume that God did not hear or will not answer.

We may take as our model Jesus' parable of the widow who came to court asking for justice day after day; finally the judge relented just to get rid of her (Luke 18:1-8). Many read this parable and see God in the role of this unjust judge. We take the place of the widow, trying to argue God into submission through prayer. Ruminating on the problem this way erodes faith by enforcing the sense that we really do not trust God.

Actually, if we take the persistent widow as our model, we are missing Jesus' point. He says God is not like that judge: "I tell you, he will *quickly* grant justice to them." Sanford's approach embodies a better understanding of Jesus' parable: we assume God has heard and is working for our good, and so we start giving thanks

> *I say a prayer of the utmost simplicity. . . . And I make in words little pictures of thankful expectation that He is thus entering and healing the soul. Why should I not give thanks? Is not the healing of the soul the very purpose of His holy sacrifice on Calvary? Is it not, then, His will and the will of the Father? What could stop it?*
>
> THE HEALING GIFTS OF THE SPIRIT

before the answer is complete. We should not assert that we believe when we do not—lying to ourselves can't nurture real faith—but there is much to be thankful for in what we know to be true. We can thank God for creating us "fearfully and wonderfully," with bodies that have already recovered from many illnesses. We can thank God for physicians and nurses whose insights and actions help the process. We can thank God for being at work in our loved ones' lives even in the midst of illness and even before we prayed. Now that we have prayed, there is still more to be thankful for. We can thank God for hearing and understanding, and working all things together for good.

Thankfulness shifts the weight of our attention. Worried repetition of the request nurtures obsession with the problem. Giving thanks fills our attention with the truth of God's goodness, mercy and power—and that is the stance of trust. Sanford has us building our faith, brick by trustworthy brick.

Step three: Be present and focus on God. Sanford recommends a couple of additional things so consistently that we should think of them as formal steps. She calls us to be present to the person who needs healing and to focus our attention on God as we pray.

Sanford does not fit many people's stereotype of a healer. Her healing ministry was not performance. It came in the context of pastoral care in homes and hospital rooms. Like the Christian life in general, her ministry of healing was all about love exercised in relationship, with genuine attentive presence. It generally included conversation to build a supportive connection, and prayer with laying on of hands. This almost required being physically present to pray for healing. If that could not happen, as when a group was praying for someone in another location, she made arrangements for someone to be at the bedside.

While present with the sick person, the focus was to be on God—certainly not on the person praying, but not even on the sick person. Sanford advises those praying for someone's healing not to try to think too hard or put their prayers into perfect words. She tells of receiving this advice from someone more experienced with healing when she was dealing with a challenging situation. Her adviser told her simply to be with the sick boy and lay her hands on his head, knowing that God is God and that God is present. She gives the same advice to others.

I find this excellent advice, because it is surprisingly faith building. When I take up her challenge to make a specific request, I often seem to try to make the answer come by the force of my words. Somehow it feels like the answer to prayer depends on me and my skillful praying, instead of on the generous love of God. I need Sanford's reminder that "Christ is the healer. No human being has the power to heal."

One night, as I worried over my nineteen-month-old son's stomach flu, I found myself by his crib, praying. I followed Sanford's advice: I put my hand on his back and simply thought of God. I sensed nothing miraculous happening, but I did let go of my usual attempt to control the situation with words. My trust in God was restored, my faith strengthened. I don't know if my son felt better, but I did. Sanford would probably say it left me more capable of participating in God's healing work: "The essence of all healing is to become so immersed in the Being of God that one forgets oneself entirely. And the most successful prayers are those in which the one who prays never thinks of himself at all."

It may sound odd to refer to "successful prayers," but her measure of success is not God's answer. She looks instead to our ability to take the focus off ourselves, so that we can be fully present with the person who needs prayer and the God who alone can heal. That builds faith—and it builds Christian character better than an approach that makes the person praying feel powerful.

Step four: Make it a joyful game. This final step might better be described as a stance that we should take toward the whole process. Sanford tells the sick and their would-be healers that they should not take the process too terribly seriously. We should not be flippant—healing is God's holy work—but we should be joyful. She is convinced that "joy is the heavenly 'O.K.' on the inner life of power." As with the rest, the goal is to build faith in the person who is praying: "When our belief is weak, the act of rejoicing and giving thanks will awaken our faith."

To nurture this light touch, she turns prayer into a game. She told one sick boy that when they prayed, they were "playing a little pretend-game." And she warns those who want to pray for others, "If we try this as a solemn duty, it may not work. Prayer needs wings of joy to fly upon. But if we do it happily and spontaneously, as a sort of game, we will often see it work right before our eyes."

USING YOUR IMAGINATION IN PRAYER

Thus far, nothing too controversial: Draw close to God, ask for help and give thanks, think about God, and lighten up. It all makes sense. But what will make prayer into this holy play? The answer is in Sanford's specific approaches that some find troubling: her use of imagination and visualization. Some find these practices troublingly similar to things in New Age and "prosperity gospel" teachings. I can understand the similarities, but I am convinced that they are tangential rather than substantial. Wrongly understood or wrongly used, any tool is dangerous. A hammer can kill, but most people have no problem using one to drive a nail. Rightly understood, Sanford's imaginative tools do not contradict a biblical faith. In fact, they build that faith.

Imagining the completion of healing. Sanford's most prominent imaginative tool is to visualize the person you are praying for in a healthy state. She once found herself unable to pray successfully for a particular person and sought advice from someone more experienced. The woman exclaimed, "Oh my dear, you're seeing them sick." Then the prescription: "When you think of someone . . . you must learn to see him *well.*" Sanford learned that we should use our "creative imagination" to make "a definite and detailed picture" of the person strong and healthy, focusing hard on this until it comes up spontaneously when we pray. It replaces the picture of the sickness or injury. Then we can ask Jesus to come and bring about the new life we are picturing, even imagining Christ within the person.

A man who had spent years in a New Age group before becoming a Christian reacted strongly against this. Sanford seemed to be teaching the secular spirituality in which visualizing changes is expected to bring them about. Yet Sanford herself does not teach that visualization causes healing. Her point is that "harnessing the imagination and training the will, one can arouse and build his faith." She uses imagination to change the person who is praying, increasing the faith that Scripture says is needed for prayer.

How does visualizing the completed healing build faith? It reverses another of the faith-corroding things that often happen when we pray: focusing our minds on the illness puts all our attention on the problem, nurturing worry. In a group in which I was teaching on Sanford's approach, several objected to her use of visualization. One member had recently broken her leg, and others were praying for her. I said, "Okay, try to pray for her but *don't* picture her broken leg." It was impossible. We already employ visualization and imagination in our prayers. When we pray for someone, they pop up before our mind's eye. We automatically think about what needs healing—and soon we are thinking really, really hard about the infection or the cancer, or vividly picturing the tubes and monitors over their hospital bed and worrying.

Sanford would have us substitute the hopeful picture of health restored. As we pray for the woman whose leg we know is broken, we imagine it strong. We can picture a depressed person joyful or see someone flattened by a fever conscious and clear-minded. Picturing the person whole and well prevents us from ruminating on the problem and directs our hearts toward hope and trust.

It is also a way to be very clear and specific about what we are asking God to do—more clear than words. As Sanford put it to someone who wondered why he should use his imagination, "No matter what you want to make, you first have to see it in your mind. Could you make a table if you didn't first see in your mind the kind of table you're going to make?" We do not cause a healing the way we make a table. But what our mind pictures is what we are really asking God for, just as we might take to a carpenter a scale drawing of a table we want built. Instead of being divided, with our mouths asking for health while our minds focus powerfully on illness, faith grows as we ask with our whole being.

I would create in my mind a definite and detailed picture of each person for whom I prayed, seeing the whole body radiant and free and well, with light in the eyes and color in the cheeks and a swinging rhythm in the walk. . . . I would hold this picture until it came to me spontaneously and naturally—until when I prayed for the person who had been ill I would see him well instantly, not by an act of will but by the joyful and triumphant belief that it was so.

THE HEALING LIGHT

Imagining the process of healing. Sanford's second kind of imaginative work is to picture the processes of healing taking place. She visualizes this in a couple ways. The most important of these, I think, prompts the title of her book *The Healing Light*. Here is her own explanation: "When we ask for the indwelling of God's Holy Spirit in the body, let us think of that part of the body that most needs His life. Let us imagine His light and life glowing there like a fire, shining there like a light." It is pretty simple. Praying for someone's congested lungs?

Picture God's holy light shining in and around his or her chest. She practices this internally when praying as she lays on hands, and she puts it into the words of her prayers, saying "I give thanks that the shining of the Holy Spirit is restoring harmony and order to all the glands and organs. . . . I rejoice that at this moment Thy healing light is removing all pain from the spine and filling the back with new vigor and life."

This use of imagination allows her to pray clearly about something well beyond human understanding: the way God actually does the work of healing. Though it is a separate kind of visualization, she can combine it with visualizing the completed healing, as when she was instructing a soldier with a broken leg. She told him to picture both the completed healing and the light of God's healing presence: "See the bone all built in and the flesh strong and perfect around it. And play like you see a kind of light shining in it—a sort of a blue light, like one of these Neon signs, shining and burning and flowing all up and down the leg."

As well as imagining the light of God's presence, Sanford had people picture their body's natural healing processes at work. She imagined bones knitting back together, muscles growing in strength or leaky heart valves coming into proper working order. Or, as with one little boy who was battling a deadly infection, she had people enter conversation with their germs. The boy's summary of the process, a year later when fighting a mere cold, was "I've got a fever now, but that's just the healing things in me doing what God and me told 'em to do and killing the germs." A few decades later, in the age of video games, Sanford might have had people see their white blood cells as the old Pac-Man character, traveling through the blood stream, gobbling up the pac-dots and ghosts of infections or tumors.

One student found Sanford was saying things similar to what she had learned as "complementary medicine" when undergoing treatment for cancer. What complementary medicine used to encourage cooperation of mind and body, Sanford, decades earlier, was using to bring the heart and mind toward trust and participation in God's healing.

Imagining the reason for healing. A third way that Sanford uses imagination is to visualize the reason for which one is praying for healing—picturing the good things that will be possible only because healing happens. This can easily be confused with picturing the completed healing, but is actually distinct from that, requiring a bit more thought. When she was first teaching prayer as a "pretend-game" with a little boy who she says had a "leaky heart," she told him,

> Pretend you're a big guy going to High School and you're on the football squad. Shut your eyes and see yourself holding the ball and running ahead of all the other fellows. "Gee, look at that guy!" the other kids will say. "Just look at him run! Gee, he's strong! I bet he's got a strong heart!" Then you say, "Thank you, God, because that's the way it's going to be." Will you play that game every night, right after you say your going-to-bed prayers?

To this little boy, a heart valve was probably a pretty vague concept. On the other hand, playing football in high school must have looked like the peak of health and success. Playing football would be the purpose for the healing; it is the life he would want to live if the healing were to happen.

There is an important tool here, but it will look different in the case of each person we pray for. When we pray for someone to be healed, we need to ask what will be possible if God brings about a complete healing, and picture that. Think about the life that this person is called to—what they do when they are living as God created them to live. A sick mother worries not only about her own body but also about the welfare of her children. Picture her fulfilling her calling: joyfully playing with the children, cooking meals for them, providing for them financially, caring in ordinary ways. That is what the healing is for. If a minister is sick, you could picture him or her preaching and leading vibrant worship, organizing a service project or caring for someone who is grieving. In our imagination we describe the person doing whatever the person is called to do as ministry, whatever the person is gifted for in this life, whatever brings them joy and fulfillment. We picture it in our minds, and we paint that picture in our words.

This has a way of taking our minds off worry, and even off healing, so that we hold the person in our heart in joy, thankful for their role in God's world. More importantly, it puts the whole process of healing into larger perspective. These things—life and love, faithful service and useful work—are surely God's will. Picturing them allows us to pray with the confidence Jesus intended when he taught us to pray "Your will be done."

MAKING GOOD USE OF SANFORD'S TEACHING

Using the imagination may be more helpful to some than to others. For some, getting a clear picture of God at work can feel like putting our weight down in trust, letting go of worry and putting healing in God's hands. For others, not so much. It can seem to some that all this visualization tempts them to think they are to make healing happen by their own powers. If so, it is probably better to revert to Sanford's earlier lessons about drawing close to God, moving from request to thanksgiving, being lovingly present with the person we are praying for and turning our attention to God, who is present too.

I hope, though, that this summary of her basic approach to prayer for healing will prompt some to dive in and read her works. I have based what I have said on her most famous book, *The Healing Light*, which deals most fully with physical healing. She also wrote *The Healing Gifts of the Spirit*, *The Healing Power of the Bible*, an autobiography called *Sealed Orders* and numerous other books.

Over the course of her career, Sanford's writing became more sober, but the topics she treated became more controversial. As a result, no matter where people start, they may find difficulties. I promised to return to the problematic parts, so here we go. I hope to help readers get around some of the problems and hold on to the good things.

The first challenge is her lack of subtlety. Sanford was a lifelong Christian, a child of Presbyterian missionaries in China and the wife of an Episcopal priest, but she was not a trained theologian. She made unorthodox assertions, like saying we are "part of God" (rather than creatures distinct from our Creator) and that our body is the image of God (rather than tracing the image of God to aspects of our inner nature). And she referred painfully often to prayer as "thought vibrations," sounding as if they affected other people directly rather than through God, who hears and answers. At better moments, though, she emphasized that Jesus is our model and teacher, and made strong statements that only God heals. If a person is looking for a theologian's sympathetic treatment of healing, he or she will do better with MacNutt, who earned a Ph.D. in theology and taught in a seminary for several years. On the other hand, if he or she starts out with the assumption that healing is irrational, unorthodox or generally wacky, McNutt won't be agreeable either.

Scholars of other disciplines can find things to object to in Sanford as well. As a historian, I cringe when she tells miracle stories that sound like folklore and makes interpretive leaps even when telling of her own experiences. Physicians and psychologists are likely to object when she writes with absolute confidence on matters in their fields. The key is to look past the overconfidence prompted by her zeal and listen for valuable insights.

Some will stumble on assertions that sound like virtually all ailments can and should be healed by prayer. Sanford can write as if lack of healing is our fault for not being close enough to God. It can sound too much like the comfortless counsel of telling the sick or grieving that God would heal if only they had real faith or more faith. We feel judged and rejected, whether by Christians or by God.

Sanford also makes bold predictions:

> One plain fact I dare to state: as more and more of us see God, live in harmony with Him and show forth His perfection in our bodies, minds and spirits, the "normal" processes of growth, maturity, old age and death will be altered. It will be possible for one who daily receives from God his spiritual sustenance to live without illness or decay for a longer and longer period of time.

She is speaking more of the coming kingdom than of present reality. She acknowledges that "in certain very difficult cases there are adjustments to the laws of God that cannot be made perfectly in this lifetime." This is a mild statement when the human mortality rate hovers perilously close to 100 percent. In other passages, she is more sober, commenting on what is and is not likely to be healed and speaking positively of death as a doorway to life. But one has to push past the eschatology to find the pastoral wisdom.

Others trip over her constant portrayal of prayer as "scientific," arguing that prayer works through God's laws as through laws of nature: "Someday we will understand the scientific principles that underlie the miracle working powers of God, and we will accept His intervention as simply and naturally as we do the radio." Her technological analogies lead to troubling theological implications: After noting that when the iron does not heat up, we do not cry out, "Oh, electricity, please come into my iron and make it work!" she concludes, "the same principle is true of the creative energy of God. The whole universe is full of it, but only the amount of it that flows through our own beings will work for us." We do need to draw close to God, but can we say the sovereign Creator of the universe should "work for us"? There is an apparent irreverence.

But we have to remember that she wrote at a time when science seemed to validate truth and promised to solve all our problems.

All this makes it easy to miss what is more crucial: Agnes Sanford really knew how to pray for healing. Even without theological training, she was asked to teach and write extensively on the topic. That is good, since we need to learn. Even those who do not have or want the charismatic gift of healing can be glad for new ways to pray for people who are suffering.

Some feel at home in Sanford's way of praying. They feel that Jesus' ministry of healing is the heart of the gospel and that Sanford has shown a way to participate in it. Others will have trouble with Sanford's teaching no matter what I say here, whether because they see New Age parallels or because they have watched good and faithful Christians pray for healing while they suffered and died. If Sanford's approach is not for you, that is just fine. One point of looking at ten different ways that Christians pray is that you figure out which ones do not suit you and which ones do.

Whether we expect miracles or feel skeptical about them, we still need to talk to God when we are ill and when those we love are suffering. Sanford can help with that; she can help us draw close to God, to ask for what we need and give thanks that God is working, to meditate on the presence of God and to pray in a joyful, playful way. And along the way, she can help us use the imagination God gave us to ask with clarity, picturing the ways God is at work and what healing will allow the sick person to do in the world.

Sanford's approach does not guarantee that God will answer yes to what we ask—nor is it meant to. But when we look closely, we can see that her ways of praying really can build confident faith. If they draw us close to God and allow us a sense of participation in God's activity in the world, they may even nurture a kind of holiness.

PRAYING WITH
ANDREW MURRAY

The Ministry of Intercession

Beloved fellow-Christians! God needs, greatly needs, priests who can draw near to Him, live in His presence, and by their intercession draw down the blessings of His grace on others. And the world needs, greatly needs, priests who will bear the burden of the perishing ones, and intercede on their behalf.

Be a priest, *only* priest, *all* priest! Seek now to walk before the Lord in the full consciousness that you have been set apart for the holy Ministry of intercession. This is the true blessedness of conformity to the image of God's Son.

ANDREW MURRAY,
With Christ in the School of Prayer

When I told people I was writing this book, I was surprised how often they asked, "Are you going to have a chapter on Andrew Murray?" Murray (1828-1917), a Scottish-educated Dutch Reformed missionary pastor from South Africa, is someone many Protestants read when they become serious about prayer. He was certainly serious about it. In language that may sound dated, but in tones that ring with sincerity, he taught that prayerlessness was the great problem in the church, holding back spiritual health and growth. He encouraged taking up prayer as a vocation. He clearly lived what he taught.

The kind of prayer Murray cared about was intercession: asking God to do things for others and especially asking God to further the work of evangelism. He was active in the great century of Protestant evangelical missions when, whether at home or at outposts around the world, Christians committed themselves to prayer. They fervently begged God to prepare the hearts of nonbelievers and to send believers out to reap the harvest. Preachers called for conversion and strove for revival, but they knew nothing would happen except through prayer. Prayer would move God to work within those who heard so that the gospel could have its saving effect.

FAMILIAR TERRITORY
Many readers today hear in Murray's writings the familiar sounds of home—though home can take on a range of meanings from "peace and comfort" to "dysfunctional family." He embodies several things that have become standard assumptions about prayer. First is the idea that intercession is the very definition of prayer, or at least the main kind of prayer. Even when people describe it as conversation with God, many can hardly talk about prayer that is not "praying for something." As I have tried to emphasize, this is by no means the only Christian definition of prayer; it is just the one that gets immediate resonance today.

When we look at Murray's best-known book, *With Christ in the School of Prayer*, a number of other features are so familiar they can slip down like honey. Murray looks to the Bible for instruction on prayer. Within the Bible he looks to Jesus as the most important teacher; that seems a good move since Jesus is God incarnate. Murray tries to examine everything Jesus specifically taught about prayer, as well as examples of Jesus himself praying. He turns these texts into a curriculum for Christ's school in thirty-one chapters for thirty-one days—a tidy month of lessons. It foreshadows a popular kind of devotional book and a prominent kind of church program.

Murray has a simple, straightforward approach when interpreting biblical texts: he takes them literally. He urges his readers not to let their rational minds get in the way with objections. Better, he thinks, to just take Jesus at his word: "Let us beware of weakening the Word with our human wisdom." Murray presents all this in the ringing tones of a preacher, making a heart-moving appeal rather than an intellectual argument. Some of the terms he uses here and elsewhere have become commonplace, at least in some circles. For example, he is the earliest person I have found to use the term "prayer warriors" for people committed to intercession, and he frequently discusses the "power of prayer."

I think Murray is impressive, but not for these familiar features. Much of what I have mentioned could actually use some critical reflection: Jesus does not necessarily give the complete picture of biblical teaching on prayer, and the more influential theologians of Christian history (Luther, Calvin and Augustine, to name just three discussed in this book) often interpreted passages of the Bible in ways that were metaphorical rather than literal. God is a rock, says the psalmist, but you can't analyze his mineral content. I will discuss some of the potential dangers as we go along, but more importantly, I want to point out some of the genuine wisdom of this influential teacher on a very important type of prayer.

Murray has ways to help us grow in intercession, tools developed in a lifetime of study and practical experience. That is good, because we all need to pray for specific things—even those who favor contemplative prayer. Beyond that, he calls us to give far more weight to prayer than Protestants are prone to do. Intercession, he tells us, is a core expression of Christian identity, an aspect of sharing the work of Christ in the world. He is not trying to help us do a better job of praying when and if we occasionally pray. He is helping us live a life in which prayer is the heart of our calling.

> *Prayer is in very deed the pulse of the spiritual life. It is the great means of bringing to minister and people the blessing and power of heaven. Persevering and believing prayer means a strong and an abundant life.*
>
> THE PRAYER LIFE

MURRAY'S BASIC METHOD

A superficial reading of Murray's books could lead some to a caricature of his method: Intercession is key, so ask God to do your will. Persistence is key, so spend more time asking. Faith is key, so pretend you really believe God will answer. God has promised, so tell God you will not take no for an answer. Murray does not really go there; actually, his starting point is a humble heart devoted to doing God's will in everything.

Superficial reading can also lead to problems and paradoxes: Murray spends a great deal of time on texts where Jesus promises that if we have faith, God will do whatever we ask in prayer—virtually anything, including throwing a mountain into the ocean. It sounds appealing, but common sense sees that two equally faith-filled Christians can pray for the exact opposite things; we need God to sort it out and do what is best. And yet, it can sound like Murray is saying if God does not answer "Yes!" it is our fault, as when he says, "where there is true faith, it is impossible but the answer must come." Frustration follows, because we can't create real faith by sheer willpower. However, if we read with care, we see that Murray himself does not take Jesus' teachings in quite such problematic directions.

Murray's writings are inspiring, but he is no more systematic about his subject than Jesus, whose scattered words he interprets. We have to find the patterns and discern the steps we might follow. In another thirty-one-day prayer program appended to another book, *The Ministry of Intercession*, he tells us, "The best way of learning to do a thing—in fact the only way—is *to do it*." It sounds vaguely prophetic of a shoe ad, but "*do it*" makes a good starting place.

Murray does not present an academic theology of prayer, which is fine, since analyzing prayer will not make you good at praying. He wants to help with the actual practice. I see Murray teaching two methods: a basic method of practical steps and a much more important set of steps we could think of as the advanced method. He does not present the steps of his basic method in order, but six pieces of his practical advice seem to me particularly helpful.

Start small. We have to learn and grow toward being competent at intercession. Murray writes, "Begin by setting apart some time every day, say ten or fifteen minutes, in which you say to God and to yourself, that you come to Him now as intercessor for others. Let it be after your morning or evening prayer, or any other time." Notice that he does not think we are up to spending hours at it to begin with. Notice as well, though, that he assumes we are already people who pray. Intercession is a particular skill or ministry for someone committed to a life of prayer. Start with a short, regular time to practice the specific work of intercession, apart from confession, praise or other important kinds of prayer.

Pray local. "Just like the Lord, each believing intercessor has his own immediate circle for whom he first prays. Parents have

their children, teachers their pupils, pastors their flocks, all
workers their special charge, all believers those whose care lies
on their hearts." None of us is individually responsible for the
welfare of the world. Our intercession should start with those to
whom we are close.

Be specific. "While, on the one hand, the heart must be en-
larged at times to take in all, the more pointed and definite our
prayer can be the better." If you pray for, say, the coming of the
kingdom of God, you will not be able to know whether God answered. On the other hand, if you ask God to help your friend to
find a job or come to Christ, you can see when it happens, grow in
faith and give thanks.

Be biblical. As John puts it, "If we ask anything according to his
will, he hears us" (1 John 5:14). Murray does not think this means
our prayers are measured against a mysterious hidden will of God.
It means we should use the Bible to know clearly what God's will
is. Though there is, he says, a secret will of God, "it is not with this
will of God, but His will as revealed in His Word that we have to
do in prayer. . . . Whatever [one] asks within the limits of that revealed will, he can know to be according to the will of God and he
may confidently expect."

Praying for what the Bible says to pray for is also simply obedi-
ent. Scripture tells us clearly to pray for a number of things. Murray summarizes the list, saying we should pray for the community
of faith and all humanity, as well as "for kings and all rulers; for all
who are in adversity; for the sending forth of laborers; for those
who labor in the gospel; for all converts; for believers who have
fallen into sin; for one another in our own immediate circles." The
list could go on.

Watch for answers. In each of the thirty-one days of lessons in
the appendix to *The Ministry of Intercession*, Murray provided
suggestions of what to pray for and how to pray. After each one,
he left several blank lines to write down our requests so that we

can take note of God's answers: "It is of extreme importance that we should prove that God hears us, and to this end take note of what answers we look for, and when they come . . . plead for the blessing. And expect and look for its coming, that you may praise God." Many before and since have recommended keeping such a prayer log to build faith.

Keep at it. "In quiet, persistent, and determined perseverance [faith] continues in prayer and thanksgiving until the blessing come." Murray says we need to persevere with our requests. His Reformed understanding of providence convinced him that God is at work within us as we pray, as well as in the people we pray for. So, he taught, if our prayer meets all the biblical conditions for prayer and God does not answer, God is working on our character. Continuing to ask, trying to trust that God will finally answer, builds faith, while God's delay in answering exercises patience.

THE ADVANCED METHOD

Utilizing the six bits of advice outlined above, anyone can begin to practice intercessory prayer. However, though they are good advice and true to Murray's teaching, I think he would find them inadequate. He called people to something deeper and richer. Throughout his writing, these small, practical steps are intermingled with three giant leaps that amount to a more advanced method—or, Murray might say, the true foundation on which the basic practice of intercession should be built.

Leap one: Make a core commitment to holiness. The crucial first step is to make a radical commitment to live in total devotion to God—to be, in Murray's old-fashioned language, "a wholly consecrated vessel." This is necessary because "what our prayer avails depends on what we are and what our life is." This comes up as he discusses the biblical conditions of prayer that can expect an answer from God. He does not make a simplistic call for perfect faith. Nor does he describe claiming the power and promises of God in the way some do, making prayer sound like an arrogant assertion of our rights. In some passages, he can seem to have fallen into those dangerous waters but, read carefully and in context, he calls us to something much more serious: "It will not be difficult to say what is needed to live such a life of prayer. The first thing is undoubtedly the entire sacrifice of the life to God's kingdom and glory." The real condition of right prayer, according to Murray, is holy life—a life dedicated to serving and glorifying God.

This is potent stuff—somewhere between the refreshing spray from a sprinkler on a hot day and a bucket of water over your head. It has always seemed to me a true and admirable way to describe being a real Christian, though Murray speaks in the language of another era. His kind of discipleship is a high calling, demanding our whole being. It is so deeply countercultural that it is rarely preached today.

This is also Murray's way of resolving Jesus' seemingly too-generous promises to hear and answer every prayer: the promises come with strict and challenging conditions. "In all God's intercourse with us, the promise and its conditions are inseparable." He would keep us humble, far from selfishly thinking we can grab God's promises for ourselves. When Jesus says, "I will do whatever you ask in my name, so that the Father may be glorified in the Son" (John 14:13), Murray says Jesus is promising on the condition that we intend to glorify the Father by what we ask. "The glory of the Father must be the aim and end, the very soul and life of our prayer." He may be playing with the grammar a bit (Jesus seems really to say that he will *answer* so that the Father will be glorified, not that our request must *aim* to glorify the Father), but Murray is pointing our hearts in the right direction.

As he points out, Jesus would not let people ask on the authority of his own name unless they were the kind of people who would pray for what he himself would want: "No one would give another the free use of his name without first being assured that his honour and interest were as safe with that other as with himself." Ending a prayer "In Jesus' name, amen" means being attuned to Christ and asking what is true to his nature. Jesus answers the prayers that are, in fact, his will. This does not discourage Murray, as if prayer is useless. It increases his desire for holiness, as he himself calls out in prayer, "Lord Jesus! Let Thy Spirit dwell in me, and fill me. I would, I do yield my whole being to His rule and leading. . . . Lord Jesus! O teach me by Thy Holy Spirit to pray in Thy Name."

Leap two: Abide in Christ. Many make commitments to follow Jesus and live his way, but then find their passion fades over time. Murray's second step is designed to nurture that core commitment to holiness so that it remains the driving force of our lives: we need to draw close to Christ and remain in his presence. This comes out as he articulates the conditions for answered prayer. He quotes John 15:7—"If you abide in me, and my words abide in you, ask for whatever you wish, and it will be done for you"—noting that the promise is unlimited. However, he also notes that the unlimited promise comes with the simple, natural condition: "*If* you abide." Our prayers go unanswered when we are not living close to Jesus, in the abiding love that expresses itself in full obedience. "It is as our faith grows into obedience," Murray says, "and in obedience and love our whole being goes out and clings itself to Christ, that our inner life becomes opened up, and the capacity is formed within of receiving the life, the spirit, of the glorified Jesus, as a distinct and conscious union with Christ and with the Father." The person in union with Christ is the one whose prayer is answered.

For Murray, even faith as a condition of answered prayer does not mean simply believing that the thing we ask will come to pass or believing factually that the promise of God is true. The faith needed is abiding in Christ. When Jesus says to have faith in God, Murray explains,

> That is, let thine eye be open to the Living God, and gaze on Him, seeing Him who is Invisible. . . . So believing God is just looking to God and what He is, allowing Him to reveal His presence, giving Him time and completely yielding the whole being to take in the full impression of what He is as God, the soul opened up to receive and rejoice in the over-shadowing of His love.

We are to trust in God personally, but note that it is expressed in looking toward God—the contemplative gaze. Surprisingly, Murray is in part a contemplative, sometimes even a bit of a mystic. He teaches that if we would abide in Christ, living out our commitment to holiness, we should be contemplatives too.

Just in case that seems a stretch for an evangelical missionary in the Reformed tradition, I will quote another passage: "Just place yourself before, and look up into, His face; think of His love, His wonderful, tender, pitying love. . . . The Father's loving heart will give light and warmth to yours." The gaze leads to union, as he himself prayed: "It is Thyself living in me as in the Father, that alone can satisfy me. It is Thyself, my Lord, no longer before me and above me, but one with me, and abiding in me; it is this I need, it is this I seek."

Murray speaks startling, much-needed words in a culture of nominal faith and culturally approved selfishness. If we read him to figure out how to get God to answer our prayers, he tells us that we need to slow down and spend time in God's company. Murray affirms that for intercession to be fitting, we need an ongoing, life-changing encounter with God. The tone of ringing sincerity makes it seem clear that he is calling us to nothing more than he has practiced for a long time. He has drawn near, abiding in Christ with the gaze of contemplation, and he calls us, too, to spend years and years, as he puts it, "simply looking at God."

Leap three: Joined with Christ, take up his priestly ministry. Building on this union with Christ, Murray invites us to a third great leap: we are to take up intercession as our way of sharing in the very work of Christ. Like Luther, Murray draws on 1 Peter 2:5, where Christians are declared to be "a holy priesthood." According to Hebrews, Christ is our great high priest, and one role of a priest is to intercede with God for the people. Our high priest has ascended to heaven, and there, according to Hebrews 7:25 and Romans 8:34, his role is to intercede for us. Murray presents intercession as prayer's highest form, because it is Christ's own ministry. Now, in union with Christ, we share his ministry of intercession.

I encounter many Christians who interpret "the priesthood of all believers" to mean that each of us can approach God directly without need for any human priest. Murray, like Luther, taught the opposite: priests are absolutely necessary. Each of us needs a priest, and each of us must be a priest for others. Luther emphasized preaching as a priestly act, speaking for God to the people, whether in church or when we tell a neighbor the good news of Christ; we all need a human mediator to tell us the gospel. Murray emphasizes another side: the priest speaks for the people to God. "God needs, greatly needs, priests," Murray says, "who can draw near to Him, who live in His presence, and by their intercession draw down the blessings of His grace on others. And the world needs, greatly needs, priests who will bear the burden of the perishing ones, and intercede on their behalf."

We might debate whether God really needs our help, but Murray seems on solid ground in saying we are called to intercession. We certainly all need others praying for us, weak and broken as we are on our own. Murray aims at something higher and more mysterious, with intercession not only our personal calling but also the ultimate sharing in Christ and his work. "Seek now to walk before the Lord in the full consciousness that you have been

set apart for the holy Ministry of Intercession. This is the true
blessedness of conformity to the image of God's Son."

Christ has opened the school of prayer specially to train intercessors for the great work of bringing down, by their faith and prayer, the blessings of His work and love on the world around. There can be no deep growth in prayer unless this be made our aim.

WITH CHRIST IN THE SCHOOL
OF PRAYER

We are joined to Christ, whether we think of union by faith or of our place in his body, the church. And joined to him, we share Christ's own personal ministry. Murray is not encouraging prayer in which we impose our will on God or act as if we are in control of the universe. He is helping us step into a role we should feel too humble to take, but which is inherent in the nature of our relationship to Jesus. As we take up intercession as our ministry, we are lifted up and transformed.

GETTING STARTED

When I teach on Murray, some tell me they already pray this way. Others tell me eagerly they plan to put it into practice. I confess I am a little doubtful. I do not doubt the value of Murray's teaching, but I suspect they are simply saying that they practice intercession, or want to. What I doubt is that many of us are ready for the passionate discipleship that he teaches as the foundation. But the advanced method—commitment to holiness, abiding in Christ and taking up his priestly ministry—is Murray's *real* method.

I must say also that many who are drawn to Murray's writings echo features of his theology that I find troubling—themes common in some preaching and writing on intercessory prayer today. I would hope that Christians would look at the theological implications of these things, rather than embracing them uncritically, and aim instead at the good core elements of Murray's method.

First, it is at least potentially dangerous to measure our Christian maturity by God's answers to our prayers, as Murray sometimes teaches. He is convinced that God will, finally, answer the mature Christian who prays in the right way—and the answer will be yes. This emphasizes childlike dependence on the Father's provision, and that is a biblical picture. However, other scriptural images more directly indicate maturity, such as growing into the fullness of Christ (Ephesians 4:13), being renewed in God's image (Colossians 3:10) and bearing the fruit of the Spirit (Galatians 5:22-23). These measures focus on our character, rather than on God's actions in response to our prayers. We are not always, in every sense, dependent children. We are called to grow up—to become like Jesus in all we think and do.

Second is his emphasis on the "power of prayer." It is a hard theme to miss. In the first chapter of *With Christ in the School of Prayer*, Murray mentions power more than a dozen times. He portrays the faithful, growing Christian regularly experiencing "the power of prayer." One can get the idea that the purpose of prayer is, in fact, power.

Christians should think carefully about the pursuit of personal power. Many assume that power is a good thing, but I question whether it is a worthy goal for Jesus' disciples. Yes, Jesus said we would receive power when the Spirit came, but he spoke of the power to be his witnesses (Acts 1:8). Jesus was more prone to emphasize giving up power, whether telling us to turn the other cheek (Matthew 5:38-42) or pouring out his own divine life on our behalf (Philippians 2:5-8). The Lord's power was made perfect in Paul's weakness (2 Corinthians 12:9). Better to pray in humble awe, grateful that God would take our requests into account at all. The real power of prayer, of course, is the power of God—and we know that power in the paradox of God wrapping himself in a towel and washing the feet of those he created.

A third, related worry comes when people want to be "prayer warriors." This can express an admirable passion for prayer, though the language can grate on the ears of those who would follow the Prince of Peace in the blessed way of peacemaking. It can also sound like we picture ourselves storming heaven, arguing God into submission to get our prayers answered. It makes me wonder who the prayer warriors think the enemy is. I have found Murray using the term only once, and he does not take it in these troubling directions. But he does emphasize at times a very urgent, insistent style of request that can be taken in an unhealthy direction. We need to consider whose will, in fact, is to be done.

I have great hope, though, for Christians who would practice intercession by starting where Murray starts. Prayer would look different in our lives and in our churches if we were to do as he did by working on our core commitment to holiness, consecrating ourselves to God, living according to God's will and serving God's purposes in the world. We would ask in less strident, gentler tones. We would ask for different things. The way forward is to live out this holiness by by abiding in Christ over time as Murray teaches. We need to draw close to God and ask him to be close to us in every moment. When we do that, not only will Christ be our teacher in the school of prayer, but we will also be united to Christ and able to participate in his own ministry by taking up the calling of intercession.

Perhaps the most remarkable feature of Murray's work, and what makes him a fitting conclusion for this survey of ten ways Christians pray, is that he creates a way for Protestants to consider prayer as a real vocation. Protestants have typically not provided structures and institutions for those called to a life of prayer, as do traditions with monasteries and convents. As typical of Protestants, Murray is absolutely living an "active" life, even if aspects of his practice of prayer are "contemplative." This is a Protestant theological understanding of prayer—calling on God, asking God's help—and it creates a Protestant, active kind of prayer vocation. Prayer is Murray's main calling, and his active ministry flows from it. The awe-inspiring way he portrays intercession as participation in Christ's own priestly work is again distinctly Protestant, growing from Luther's thought on believers' priesthood, and a vastly richer way of portraying prayer than is typical today. In this age when few are choosing monastic life, Murray's invitation to this particular life of prayer in the active life can be a fresh option for the Catholic and Orthodox as well.

When we have spent time abiding in Christ, learning what Jesus teaches about prayer and becoming humble enough to know we do not have it mastered, we are ready to really take up Murray's basic program: Set aside ten or fifteen minutes a day to practice intercession. Make requests for those closest to you first, then in larger circles for the church, for mission, for the world. Ask specifically—for what is really needed. Ask God for the things Scripture clearly tells us to ask for. Watch for answers, looking for the signs that God is at work around us. Keep at it; repeating our requests won't bother the God who loves us so much that he adopted us as his children. And perseverance in the face of unanswered prayer does build patience.

Go ahead. Take up the ministry of prayer. Intercession really is a ministry—Christ's own. This is no hobby to putter at. Communion with God is our great privilege in Christ. Joined to Christ, we are given the awesome and mysterious invitation to share his work: we join our voices with his in the ongoing project of redeeming God's world.

BENEDICTION

I started this book with Benedict's way of prayer. Since each hour of his divine office ends with a blessing, it seemed best for me to end with one as well. May God bless you richly as you draw near to God in prayer.

If you tried all these ways of praying, it is likely that some did not appeal to you at all. Maybe even reading about some of them was more than enough. When I teach on prayer in churches or at the seminary, people seem embarrassed if they do not like one of them. I always tell them that this is actually terrific. Part of discerning what does fit your relationship with God is discerning what does not. No one could be expected to do all of these things all the time. Probably no one would even want to. No problem. Just know that someone else will love the very form of prayer you can't connect with at all. And be glad you know that very way of praying, because someday you may find yourself in a season when what you now dislike is just the right thing.

I do hope you will try each one, though, and for long enough to really understand it from the inside. You need more than a gut reaction, either positive or negative. You will really know a way of praying only if you get past the first response, get genuinely comfortable putting it into use, even get completely bored with it, and then do it some more. That will be a good start.

Of course, few are likely to invest that much in more than a couple of approaches. But if you do find even one new way of praying here that you can stick with for the next season of your life, that will be a great gain.

FREEDOM TO EXPERIMENT

Each of the ten ways to pray discussed here is an excellent, genuinely Christian approach with deep roots. Depending on your own theological background and personality, you may find yourself more open to some and more critical of others. I certainly am. Some will surely have insurmountable theological objections to particular approaches. I hope, though, that you can move away from the kind of theological critique that rejects and condemns without a fair hearing. Better to learn from our sisters and brothers in Christ, no matter how strange some of the things they do seem to us. Each teacher discussed in this book lived an authentic Christian life, and each approach points to a living tradition of the faith. When I teach these different approaches, I love to see people open up to this possibility. Exploring prayer in a community helps: hearing each other's responses, people discover that what they would personally reject outright can be a life-changing blessing to others they know and respect.

Once you allow yourself to see all of these as authentically Christian possibilities, you can, in freedom, use them according to your personality and needs. Whether you like writing or reading, you have ways to pray. Whether you want a set pattern or an invitation to imagination, you have ways to pray. Whether you want to ask for specific things or pour out praise or sit in silence, you have ways to pray.

The discoveries can be surprising. I have mentioned some along the way: A woman who struggled academically yet found joy in studying the psalms prayerfully à la Calvin. An evangelical man who found himself to be a natural contemplative, praying happily with *The Cloud of Unknowing*. Others discovered the value of journaling or the Lord's Prayer or intercession. When my wife was spending countless hours of the day and night nursing our newborn daughter, she discovered the joy of Benedictine prayer. How, you might ask, could she flip from section to section in a breviary with a baby in her arms? Well, now you can pray the office on a smart phone, with the psalms, prayers and readings for each hour all organized for you. Finding a new way to pray that really fits is a deeply satisfying thing, whether it is for a lifetime or just for a season.

Accepting them all as valid ways for Christians to pray can also shape how you relate to others as they struggle with prayer. Whether you are a pastor or a friend, knowing that there are options helps. It can, in a way, help pastors do more of something at the core of their calling. Pastoral ministry used to be called "the cure of souls," meaning caring for people's spiritual life. Some traditions call it spiritual direction, and others call it discipling. Whatever the name, those who serve as the shepherds need to help God's flock find green pastures, with nourishment and refreshment for their ongoing relationship with God.

|||||||||||||||||||||||||||||||||||||||||||||||||||||||||||||||||||||

Sursum corda! Indulge mihi, precor, has balbutiones. Semper in meis orationibus et es et eris. Vale. (*Lift up your hearts! Permit me, I pray you, these stammerings. You are ever in my prayers and ever will be. Farewell.*)

C. S. LEWIS TO DON GIOVANNI CALABRIA, DECEMBER 26, 1951

|||||||||||||||||||||||||||||||||||||||||||||||||||||||||||||||||||||

It is easy for those in professional ministry to become completely absorbed in the administrative demands of church life. It so often happens that caring for people's spiritual growth is more and more given over to those who practice spiritual direction as a specialized ministry. Spiritual direction is a wonderful ministry, but it would be even better if pastors could focus their energy on it too. Many people who would never think of seeking a spiritual director have an established relationship with their pastor. I hope, and indeed I pray, that knowing the wide variety of authentically Christian ways of praying will put the question of spiritual growth at the front of pastors' minds. Whether planning a sermon or meeting with the building and grounds committee, helping people grow close to God and grow up in Christ is a minister's chief calling. That starts with helping them pray. All the rest flows from that.

These "giants" of prayer have us do such radically different things that it is surprising that they have some crucial things in common. They all are convinced that prayer is of ultimate importance. Whether they call it the work of God or the chief work of faith or our participation in Christ's priestly calling, it is at the heart of who we are and what we do. If, even after exploring these ancient and recent traditions, you still feel like a beginner, that is fine. All seem to agree that prayer is not easy. It takes time to learn it, whether they frame it as an experiment in seeing God at work, a private engagement with the text of Scripture or a corporate discipline within monastic walls. The key is to pick an approach that fits for the time being and to keep coming back to it.

Surprisingly often these teachers, with personalities and theologies as different as Agnes Sanford and the anonymous author of *The Cloud of Unknowing,* affirm the same goal for the journey: the presence of God. No matter whether we frame our prayer as a request for mercy or for daily bread, for healing or for God's work in the world, this is ultimately what we seek. Nothing more could be sought, since nothing is greater than the God who made us and redeemed us in Christ. We seek the presence of God. And whenever we pray, no matter how we pray, if we truly pray, we find we are in God's presence.

APPENDIX 1

Using This Book in Small Groups and Church Classes

This book can be read on your own, and all the ways of praying can be explored individually, but it can also be used in small groups and church classes of various kinds. From my experience and the experiments of my students, I suggest multi-session adult education classes, independent small-group studies, one-day retreats, youth group lessons and staff team-building sessions—any context where people want to learn to pray or where you, as a leader, think it would be useful to teach people to pray. No matter what the context is, I hope leaders will structure their group's explorations of the book so that the members practice the ways of praying described here. Simply reading and discussing the information in the book falls infinitely short of discussing our own experiences of prayer.

Some groups or church classes would be able to commit ten weeks to spend one week on each chapter of the book. In many contexts, however, it will work better to select two to four chapters and spend either one or two weeks on each. I would strongly rec-

ommend not trying to do more than one chapter per week so that
class members can practice the method of prayer taught in the assigned chapter as preparation for discussing it. Asking people to
practice two of them at once will probably not lead to clear discussion and may lead to people not praying either way.

SELECTING A USEFUL SET OF CHAPTERS

As you think about going through a few chapters of the book with
a group, I recommend reading through the book and thinking
about the various possible groupings. You would do well to find a
set of chapters that fits the needs of your group because they connect to your tradition, because they have something in common
that scratches a particular itch or because they will stretch people
in some healthy way. Here are a few possibilities:

1. Choose one of the four parts of the book. Each one provides
   two or three chapters with a clear common thread.

2. If you want to explore Catholic examples, whether your group
   is Catholic or not, you could do Benedict, Teresa, *The Cloud of
   Unknowing* and Ignatius.

3. If you want to explore teachers from the Reformed tradition,
   you could do Calvin, the Puritans and Andrew Murray.

4. If you are interested in models taught by women, you could do
   Teresa and Agnes Sanford.

5. If you are historically minded, you could do approaches rooted
   in the early church, including Benedict, Augustine (found in
   the Puritans chapter) and the Jesus Prayer (presented in modern form in the Pilgrim chapter).

6. Another historical grouping would be the Reformation era,
   with Luther, Calvin, Ignatius and Teresa. You could also include the Anglican tradition here, which is woven into the
   Benedict chapter.

7. Those drawn to prayer that includes writing could do Calvin and the Puritans.

8. You could also chose a pair that seem like opposite ends of a spectrum—perhaps Calvin and *The Cloud of Unknowing*, or Agnes Sanford and the Puritans.

9. You could choose three that seem like a deepening journey into ways of prayer that you are already familiar with—perhaps Martin Luther's use of the Lord's Prayer, Teresa's free conversation and Andrew Murray's intercession.

10. If your group is going to read texts by the teachers discussed in the chapters (such as the excerpts in the *Kneeling with Giants Reader*), you might choose two or three that all make use of the Lord's Prayer, which includes Martin Luther, of course, but also Benedict, Teresa and Andrew Murray.

PREPARATION AND LEADERSHIP

When promoting the class, make it clear that participants should read the first assigned chapter and practice that way of praying the week before the first session. Whether you use all the chapters or just one, I hope you will have people also read the relevant portions of the *Kneeling with Giants Reader*, the electronic book of primary source texts that accompanies this book. This is especially aimed at those using this book in college or seminary classes, but learning from the sources can be engaging and fun, and it will give a context for what is found in the chapters. Plus, my secret agenda as a historian is always to get people to read primary sources. I hope you will be interested enough in the portions I provide to seek out the books themselves on your own or with a group.

Below I will describe a hypothetical session focused on an individual chapter of the book, but it would probably be useful to have an initial session in which people share their past experiences and current understanding of prayer. Whatever the topic of that first session, the leader should note that prayer is a very intimate topic; members of the class should welcome what others share about their way of relating to God with gentleness and hospitality and treat what is shared as confidential.

If the group is led cooperatively, your task is pure facilitation. If you are the official leader or teacher, you may want to be more familiar with the readings and sometimes add clarifications about the approach to prayer as found in the book or primary source readings. The process will accomplish the most if the group agrees to work on gaining a solid understanding of texts and ideas as well as on reflecting honestly on their own experiences.

ONE HYPOTHETICAL SESSION

After opening with prayer, guide the group through questions like the following, allowing several to share on each one, but do not insist that everyone speak. In groups larger than a dozen and in smaller groups where some are dominant and others hold back, it can be useful to discuss the questions in pairs or trios first and then to share as a large group.

1. "What are your first impressions of praying this way? Share what it felt like and what was surprising."

2. "If someone who is not in this group asked you 'How does X teach that we should pray?' how would you explain his or her approach?" Another way to ask this is, "When you tried to pray according to X's instructions, what exactly did you do?" If you are the official leader, this can be a place to help people see more clearly what the actual method of prayer being taught is.

3. If the chapter has technical terms or concepts that are crucial to understanding or practicing it, ask, "What does the author appear to mean by the term Y?"

4. If the chapter makes use of something members already know from faith and life (silence in *The Cloud of Unknowing*, the

Lord's Prayer in Martin Luther, the psalms in Calvin, journaling in the Puritans, etc.), you could ask, "What role has Z played in your past experience of prayer?"

5. "Now that you have tried this for a week, what do you think might be benefits and drawbacks of praying this way?" You may find it helpful to break this into two separate questions: "What good things might happen in your Christian life if you kept this as a discipline for the next several years?" and "What strikes you as troubling or problematic about praying this way?"

Before closing the session with prayer, especially if the response to a particular approach to prayer has been negative, you may want to be prepared to note potential benefits or the importance of that way of praying for some portion of Christ's church. Likewise, if the group embraces an approach completely uncritically, it would be wise to note potential problems and raise questions. Be sure to clarify the next week's assigned reading, and encourage people to practice praying that way before the next meeting.

The context in which I most frequently teach this material is not typical: a two-semester course in a theological seminary. I am able to devote two weeks to each of the ten approaches in the book, and I can expect the participants to do their homework. Prior to the first session on a topic, I send them off with primary source readings to guide them, and they are to pray as taught in the readings. After a week, we gather in class to discuss what they found in the texts and what it was like to pray that way. At that time I also provide more direct guidance in lectures containing much that you find in these chapters, which often helps them to find the method of prayer in the primary sources they have been reading.

I find that having my students explore a way of praying the first week with guidance only from the primary sources helps them be ready to benefit from my input; they know what their questions

and objections are. Then I send them out for a second week of
prayer and reading, leading to a second session of discussion. The
two-week cycle is optimal, I find, because people often have a
much different experience in a second week of practice. They put
the method into practice differently, either because they got some
guidance or because they adapt it slightly as they become familiar
with it. Also, and more importantly, the ways of praying feel different in a second week—sometimes better, sometimes worse. If
the students had only one week and decided they could not stand
a particular approach, they might well reject something that could
have been helpful.

If your context allows a second week on each chapter, the second session could include questions like the following:

1. "What did you *do* differently this second week of praying as
   taught by *X*?"

2. "What *felt* different in this second week of praying this way,
   and why do you think it felt different?" I sometimes poll the
   group to find who liked it better and who found it less appealing in the second week.

3. "What still, or now, seems troubling about this way of praying?"

4. "What now appear to be potential benefits of praying this way?"

5. "Whether you like it for yourself or not, what kind of personality do you think this way of praying might appeal to?
   What particular life circumstances might make this a useful
   kind of prayer?"

APPENDIX 2

Putting Prayer into Practice

Whether you are using this book on your own, as part of a group or as a teacher of a class, you need ways to put each new approach to prayer into practice. What follows is a manageable summary of the type of prayer taught in each chapter and a way to try it out for a week, usually in five to fifteen minutes per day. This is just enough to become familiar with each one—an initial taste so you can begin to discern whether it might be helpful to you in the longer run.

This initial taste should not be confused with a thorough experiential knowledge. Even a second week can bring an entirely different impression, and if you invest months or years, you may be surprised by the depths that are revealed. Even within a first week of practice, you may find you want to spend longer than a quarter of an hour at prayer. That is fine, of course, and is a good eventual goal for any of these approaches. I set the initial time commitment low, knowing that for many people any dedicated time of prayer is an addition to a very busy life. With a short time commitment people are more likely to feel they are succeeding from the very beginning.

After each week with a new practice, I encourage you to spend a few minutes writing about the experience in a journal: describe what it felt like, what the potential benefits and drawbacks of praying this way appear to be, and what kind of person you think might find it a useful approach.

CHAPTER 1: Praying with St. Benedict: *The Divine Office*

Find the Benedictine hours of Lauds and Vespers in the *Kneeling with Giants Reader*, or obtain a copy of the Book of Common Prayer and locate Morning and Evening Prayer. Decide whether morning or evening is best for you, and put a fifteen-minute appointment with God in your calendar before or after work for the next week. When the time comes, find a quiet place, open to the appropriate page, and read through the "hour," praying along with the words of the liturgy. If you are using the Book of Common Prayer, as you become familiar with the order, add the relevant psalms and other Scripture readings.

CHAPTER 2: Praying with Martin Luther: *The Lord's Prayer*

Decide what time of day is best for you to pray, and put a fifteen-minute appointment with God in your calendar every day for the next week. Write out the Lord's Prayer on a card, with each clause on a separate line. When your time for prayer comes, find a quiet place. Then, confining yourself to fifteen minutes, use the lines of the Lord's Prayer as an outline, praying on each topic in your own words, whether in praise, thanks or petition. With each topic, start by praying for yourself, then move outward to your family, your church and the world. If on a particular day one petition moves you, feel free to spend the entire time on it, but move to the next one on the next day. It will help to read Luther's expositions of the Lord's Prayer in the *Kneeling with Giants Reader*.

CHAPTER 3: Praying with the Pilgrim: *The Jesus Prayer*

Decide what time of day is best for you to pray, and put a five-minute appointment with God in your calendar every day for the next week. When the time for prayer comes, find a quiet place. Then pray the Jesus Prayer for the entire time. Say it along with your breath: as you inhale, "Lord Jesus Christ, Son of God"; as you exhale, "have mercy on me." When you are comfortable with these five-minute sessions, increase the time in small increments as you see fit. Try also saying the Jesus Prayer at other times during the day, such as while walking or driving or as you turn to a new task. It will help to explore *The Pilgrim's Tale* and the *Philokalia*, starting with the portions in the *Kneeling with Giants Reader*.

CHAPTER 4: Praying with John Calvin:
Studious Meditation on the Psalms

Decide what time of day is best for you to pray, and put a fifteen-minute appointment with God in your calendar every day for the next week. Have your Bible, a notebook and a pen ready, and when the time for prayer comes, find a quiet place. Pick a psalm; it doesn't matter which one, but it's best to start out with a short one. Read through the psalm a couple of times, then turn to the questions about the text in figure 4.1 (p. 86). Pick one question from the first group, read the psalm again to try to answer it, and write a sentence or two about it in your notebook. Then do the same with one question from each of the remaining groups. Next, turn to the questions in figure 4.2 (p. 91), which relate the psalm to your life. Again, take one question from each group in turn, read the psalm to ponder the answer, and write briefly about it. If this takes more than fifteen minutes to finish, return to the same psalm the next day and pick up where you left off. It may also lead to more extensive prayer, in writing or in silence. To get a sense of what this produced in Calvin's life and to see him at work praying with the psalms, see the excerpts in the *Kneeling with Giants Reader.*

CHAPTER 5: Praying with Ignatius of Loyola:
The Prayer of the Senses

The prayer of the senses will be most useful if you have a clear sense of a question you need to talk with God about. If you do not have that clarity, there is no better way to get it than to practice the "examination of conscience," or "examen," for a week before trying the prayer of the senses. Before going to bed each night, prayerfully consider what the "consolations" and "desolations" of the day have been—the things that have helped you love God more and the things that have made God's grace seem far off. At the end of the week, consider this same question for the week as a whole and for the whole season of life you are in. Listen in your answers for a sense of where you are growing or needing to grow, for changes you want to make and for questions you need to explore.

When you are aware of the topic you need to discuss with God, find a substantial time, perhaps an hour and a half, that you can set aside for prayer. Put the appointment with God in your calendar. When the time comes, find a quiet place and have your Bible with you. Pick a narrative passage from the Gospels: Ignatius had people start with the Annunciation (Luke 1:26-38); I often have people start with the wedding at Cana (John 2:1-11). Read your passage several times—or better still, study it with care. Pray for the guidance of the Spirit, and bring your question clearly to mind.

Then, pray through the text with each sense in turn, attending to what each of your senses would have experienced if you were there, and imagine that you are indeed present in the story. Once you have prayed through all five senses, imagine yourself coming up to Mary, Jesus or another character in the story and asking your question. Imagine the response you receive, and carry on as much conversation as your prayerful imagination allows. It may help to have this conversation in writing in your journal. It would be wise to repeat the exercise later, asking the same question with one or more other passages of Scripture. To see Ignatius's own instructions for these ways of praying, go to the *Kneeling with Giants Reader*.

CHAPTER 6: Praying with St. Teresa of Ávila: *Recollection of the Presence of God*

Decide what time of day is best for you to pray, and put a ten-minute appointment with God in your calendar every day for the next week. When the time for prayer comes, find a quiet place. Take one of the biblical images of God that Teresa writes about (King, Father, Spouse, Friend) and put your attention on God in this role. Consider also what this portrait of God implies about who you are and the kind of relationship it sets up between you and God. In the quiet of your heart or aloud, speak to God in words appropriate to this relationship. You can express thanks, praise, requests or lamentations, but frame them in ways appropriate to your King, your Father, your Spouse or your Friend.

The next day, take up another of these biblical images and repeat the process. Once you have tried all four biblical portraits, you may want to try bringing some particular topic to prayer, spending a small amount of time recollecting each of the biblical images in turn. That is, within the same time of prayer, talk about the same issue with God as King, then as Father, then as Spouse, then as Friend. As Brother Lawrence shows, you can also take this practice into daily living outside set times of prayer, nurturing an awareness of God's presence. See the instructions and example of St. Teresa and the readings in the *Kneeling with Giants Reader*.

CHAPTER 7: Praying with the Puritans:
Meditation in Writing
Decide what time of day is best for you to pray, and put a fifteen-minute appointment with God in your calendar every day for the next week. When the time comes, have your journal and a pen ready, and find a quiet place. Ask God to be present with you, to listen in as you prayerfully write. On the pages of your journal, do one of the exercises described in the chapter. As John Beadle instructs, look for the actions of God in your life by writing out your spiritual autobiography, or listing the blessings you receive each day, or recording the people and things God has used in your life or the things you are asking in prayer. Or as Thomas Hooker recommends, take stock of your progress toward Christlike maturity, reflecting on your life in light of one of his "marks" or some other biblical measure. Or follow Cotton Mather's model of "spiritualizing the creatures," looking at things in the natural world, pondering biblical connections to them and looking for lessons you can draw. All of this is described in the Puritan texts in the *Kneeling with Giants Reader*, as well as demonstrated in classic form in Augustine's *Confessions*.

CHAPTER 8: Praying with *The Cloud of Unknowing*:
Contemplation in the Dark
Decide what time of day is best for you to pray, and put a five-minute appointment with God in your calendar every day for the next week. When the time comes, find a quiet place. For the full five minutes, try to turn your attention fully on God. Do not try to think about God; try instead to give your attention personally to God in love. During this time, all thoughts of things in creation need to be set aside. You do not need to start by trying to silence your mind or still your heart; rather, start by turning toward God, and as thoughts inevitably creep in, set them aside. To see this described in full, see the excerpts of *The Cloud of Unknowing* in the *Kneeling with Giants Reader*.

CHAPTER 9: Praying with Agnes Sanford:
The Healing Light

Decide what time of day is best for you to pray, and put a ten-minute appointment with God in your calendar every day for the next week. When the time comes, find a quiet place. Think of one to three people for whose healing you want to pray. The list should definitely include others, though you may also include yourself. The healing you pray for can be of any kind, but start with simple things. Remembering that your goal is to pray in ways that nurture faith, rather than to get God to do your will, spend your ten minutes each day praying according to Agnes Sanford's basic method: draw close to God; ask specifically and move to thanking God and thinking about God; maintain a joyful, playful attitude. Each time you pray for each person, use at least one of her imaginative tools: imagine the person healed rather than suffering; imagine the process of healing taking place; picture the person living the life and fulfilling the calling that healing will make possible. To get a richer sense of how this worked in Sanford's own teaching and experience, see the excerpts in the *Kneeling with Giants Reader.*

CHAPTER 10: Praying with Andrew Murray:
The Ministry of Intercession

Decide what time of day is best for you to pray, and put a ten- to fifteen-minute appointment with God in your calendar every day for the next week. When the time comes, find a quiet place. Spend at least the first five minutes asking God to help you in what I have called Murray's "advanced" method: to help you consecrate your life to God's service, to help you remain always close to Christ, to help you take up Christ's own priestly ministry of intercession and to answer your prayers in the ways that best bring God glory.

Spend the remaining time applying the steps of what I called Murray's "basic" method: speak to God about each person in your immediate circle of care, asking God to help each one in specific ways; ask specifically for the things Scripture tells us to pray for, especially that God would equip and send people to do his work in the world, for the suffering and for those who bear the responsibility in government. Keep a list of the things you are praying for, so that as you persevere in prayer, you can notice God's response. For a sense of this ministry of intercession in Murray's teaching and experience, see the excerpts in the *Kneeling with Giants Reader.*

NOTES

Chapter 1: Praying with St. Benedict: The Divine Office

page 20   "Nothing is to be preferred": *RB 1980: The Rule of St. Benedict in Latin and English with Notes*, ed. Timothy Fry (Collegeville, Minn.: Liturgical Press, 1981), 43.1-3, 72.8-11.

page 21   Benedict specified seven services: Ibid., 16.1-5.

page 27   Possibilities include translations of the *Monastic Diurnal*: Lauds, Sext, Vespers and Compline from the *Monastic Diurnal* are included in the *Kneeling with Giants Reader*.

page 29   Praying the psalms is the heart: *RB 1980*, 18.22-25.

page 33   "By searching continually": *Saint Gregory the Great: Dialogues*, trans. Odo John Zimmerman (New York: Fathers of the Church, 1959), pp. 62-63.

page 33   the whole world was gathered up before his eyes: Ibid., pp. 105-6.

page 34   "a school for the Lord's service": *RB 1980*, prologue and 4.78.

Chapter 2: Praying with Martin Luther: The Lord's Prayer

page 38   "The ordinary person, especially in the villages": Martin Luther, preface to The Small Catechism, *The Book of Concord: The Confessions of the Evangelical Lutheran Church*, ed. Robert Kolb and Timothy J. Wengert (Minneapolis: Fortress, 2000), p. 347.

page 38   "If he, the good and faithful Teacher": Martin Luther, "An Exposition of the Lord's Prayer for Simple Laymen (1519)," in *Luther's Works* (Philadelphia: Fortress, 1969), 42.21.

page 39   seventy million Lutherans: This figure comes from the Lutheran World Federation (see www.lutheranworld.org/lwf/). In 2002 the number of Lutherans was 65.4 million according to *The Encyclopedia of Christianity* (Grand Rapids: Eerdmans, 2003), s.v. "Lutheran Churches and Lutheran World Federation."

page 42   Luther had a very difficult relationship with his own father: For the classic study by a psychoanalyst, see Erik H. Erikson, *Young Man Luther: A Study in Psychoanalysis and History* (New York: Norton, 1958).

page 42   "Now of all names there is none that gains us more": Luther, "An Exposition of the Lord's Prayer," 42.22.

page 42   "Now through your mercy implant": Martin Luther, "Personal Prayer Book," in *Luther's Works* (Philadelphia: Fortress, 1969), 43.29.

page 43   "Grant us your divine grace": "Personal Prayer Book," 43:30.

page 43   "Convert those who are still to be converted": Martin Luther, "A Simple Way to Pray," in *Luther's Works* (Philadelphia: Fortress, 1969), 43.195.

page 44   "May we become your kingdom": Luther, "Personal Prayer Book," 43.32.

page 44   If we are not living as God intends: Luther, "An Exposition of the Lord's Prayer," 42.37-39.

page 44   "They are many and mighty": Luther, "A Simple Way to Pray," 43.195.

page 44   "He himself commanded us to pray like this": Luther, The Small Catechism, p. 358.

page 45   "O Father," he prayed, "do not let me": Luther, "An Exposition of the Lord's Prayer," 42.48. See the full discussion on pp. 42-49.

page 46   "Therefore, O heavenly Father, grant grace": Luther, "Personal Prayer Book," 43.34-35. See also "An Exposition of the Lord's Prayer," 42.56-58. Even early on, he is leaving behind the tradition of interpreting this "bread" as the Eucharist.

page 46   "Grant [the emperor] wisdom and understanding": Luther, "A Simple Way to Pray," 43.196-97.

page 47   "We must first forgive our debtors": Luther, "Personal Prayer Book," 43.36.

page 47   "Grant forgiveness also to those who have harmed": Luther, "A Simple Way to Pray," 43.197.

page 47   "Dear Father, I come to you and pray that you will forgive": Martin Luther, The Large Catechism, in *The Book of Concord: The Confessions of the Evangelical Lutheran Church*, ed. Robert Kolb and Timothy J. Wengert (Minneapolis: Fortress, 2000), pp. 452-53.

page 48   Luther meant something else: Luther, "Personal Prayer Book," 43.37.

page 48   "The whole world is filled with stories": Luther, "An Exposition of the Lord's Prayer," 42.74.

page 49   "Help that we may withstand excesses in eating": Luther, "Personal Prayer Book," 43.37.

page 49   "to tear us away from faith": Luther, The Large Catechism, p. 454.

page 49   Evil may seem too strong a word: Luther, "Personal Prayer Book," 43.38.

page 49   "Protect us from every bodily evil and woe": Ibid.

page 51   "I may get lost among so many ideas in one petition": Luther, "A Simple Way to Pray," 43.198.

page 51   "A prayer spoken only in behalf of oneself": Luther, "An Exposition of the Lord's Prayer," 42.60.

page 52   "Finally, mark this, that you must always speak the Amen firmly": Luther, "A Simple Way to Pray," 43.198.

Chapter 3: Praying with the Pilgrim: The Jesus Prayer

page 54   "unceasing, self-activating prayer of the heart": The Pilgrim's Tale, ed. Aleksei Pentkovsky, trans. T. Allen Smith, Classics of Western Spirituality 95 (Mahwah, N.J.: Paulist, 1999), p. 81.

page 55   "The mind needs some task which will keep it": Kallistos Ware, The Orthodox Way (Crestwood, N.Y.: St. Vladimir's Seminary Press, 1979), p. 122.

page 56   "Sit in silence and alone": Pilgrim's Tale, p. 61.

page 65   "The principal thing is to stand before God": Kallistos Ware, "Ways of Contemplation: 1. Eastern," in Christian Spirituality: Origins to the Twelfth Century, ed. Bernard McGinn et al., World Spirituality: An Encyclopedic History of the Religious Quest 12 (New York: Crossroad, 1997), p. 395.

page 59   In this cramped position, the eyes are closed: Ibid., pp. 408-9.

page 64   "I sensed a powerful urge to turn inward": Pilgrim's Tale, p. 110.

page 68   "When we are remembering our neighbor": Ibid., pp. 217-18.

page 69   Though feelings are not the goal: John Meany et al., "The Effectiveness of the 'Jesus Prayer' and Relaxation on Stress Reduction as Measured by Thermal Biofeedback," Journal of

Pastoral Counseling 19 (1984): 63-67.

page 70   "What is good, except God?" Evagrios the Solitary, "On Prayer: One Hundred and Fifty-Three Texts," in *The Philokalia: The Complete Text,* vol. 1 (London: Faber and Faber, 1979), nos. 31-33, p. 60.

pages 70-71   Lord Jesus Christ, Son of God / have mercy on me: The poem is my own.

Chapter 4: Praying with John Calvin: Studious Meditation on the Psalms

page 78   Eventually these became hefty volumes of scholarly: John Calvin, "The Author's Preface," in *Commentary on the Book of Psalms,* trans. James Anderson (1845; reprint, Grand Rapids: Baker, 1993), 1:xxxvi.

page 79   "an infallible proof of his faith": John Calvin, Psalm 3:4, in ibid.

page 79   "clamor and complaint": Calvin, Psalm 18:3, in ibid.

page 79   "bearing the cross" of obedience: Ibid., pp. xxxviii-xxxix.

page 80   Calvin taught that human beings are helpless: John Calvin, *Institutes of the Christian Religion,* ed. John T. McNeill, trans. Ford Lewis Battles (Philadelphia: Westminster Press, 1960), 1.6.1-2.

page 80   With the Spirit's illumination, we understand it: Ibid., 1.7.4. This idea has lived on in worship services in Calvin's tradition in which, prior to the reading of Scripture and the sermon, the people pray a "prayer for illumination," asking God's Spirit to guide them to the truth.

page 81   but the fourfold process: Guigo II, *The Ladder of Monks: A Letter on the Contemplative Life,* trans. Edmund Colledge and James Walsh (Kalamazoo, Mich.: Cistercian Publications, 1981), p. 67.

page 82   "Reading [*lectio*], as it were, puts food whole into the mouth": Ibid., p. 69. The Latin is found in "Lettre Sur La Vie Contemplative (L'echelle des moines)," ed. Edmund Colledge and James Walsh, Sources Chrétiennes 163 (Paris: Les Éditions du Cerf, 1970), pp. 84-86.

page 82   "Reading is the careful study of the Scriptures": Guigo II, *Ladder of Monks,* p. 68.

page 82   "wishing to have a fuller understanding of this": Ibid., p. 69.

page 82   "hammered out on the anvil of meditation": Ibid., pp. 70-71.

pages 83-84   "I count myself one of the number of those who write": *Institutes,* "John Calvin to the Reader," p. 5.

| page 94 | "call him to reveal himself as wholly present to us": Ibid., 3.20.2. |

page 94 — "call him to reveal himself as wholly present to us": Ibid., 3.20.2.

page 95 — *"Our God you are our firm protection"*: The French text of Calvin's paraphrase of Psalm 46 is in the *Ioannis Calvini Opera, quae supersunt omnia*, ed. Wilhem Baum et al. (Brunsvigae-Berolini: C. A. Schwetschke et filium, 1863-1900), vol. 6, col. 211-12. The translation of these lines is my own.

Chapter 5: Praying with St. Ignatius of Loyola: The Prayer of the Senses

page 98 — In an age before anesthetics, he endured surgery: Ignatius of Loyola, *Autobiography,* in *Ignatius of Loyola: The Spiritual Exercises and Selected Works*, ed. George E. Ganss (New York: Paulist, 1991), par. 2, p. 69.

page 99 — "any means of preparing and disposing our soul": Ibid., par. 1, p. 121.

page 101 — He wants us to look hard for where we have kept: Ibid., pars. 32-44, pp. 132-35.

page 101 — We consider these things with careful psychological analysis: Ibid., pars. 238-46, pp. 178-79. For helpful background, see also Ganss's notes 120 and 121 to this section, and par. 18, p. 128 n. 8.

page 103 — "examination of consciousness": George A. Aschenbrenner, "Consciousness Examen," in *Notes on the Spiritual Exercises of St. Ignatius of Loyola* (St. Louis: Review for Religious, 1983), pp. 175-85.

page 104 — It is also a delightful way to deepen prayer with children: For a lovely treatment of this form of the examen and its use with others or in groups, see Dennis Linn, Sheila Fabricant Linn and Matthew Linn, *Sleeping with Bread: Holding What Gives You Life* (Mahwah, N.J.: Paulist, 1995).

page 105 — "I mean that which occurs when some interior motion": Ignatius of Loyola, *Spiritual Exercises*, par. 316, p. 202.

page 105 — "is completely listless, tepid, and unhappy": Ibid., par. 317, p. 202.

page 108 — "The Preparatory Prayer is to ask God our Lord": Ibid., par. 46, p. 136.

page 109 — "see the persons, by meditating and contemplating": Ibid., par. 122, p. 151.

page 109 — "listen to what they are saying or might be saying": Ibid., par. 123, p. 151.

page 110   "sweetness and charm of the Divinity": Ibid., par. 124, p. 151.
page 110   "Using the sense of touch": Ibid., par. 125, p. 151.

Chapter 6: Praying with St. Teresa of Ávila:
Recollection of the Presence of God

page 118   "a continual conversation with Him": Brother Lawrence of
                  the Resurrection, *The Practice of the Presence of God*, trans.
                  John J. Delaney (New York: Image Books, 1977), p. 37.

page 120   "It is called recollection because the soul collects": Teresa of
                  Ávila, *The Way of Perfection*, trans. and ed. E. Allison Peers
                  (New York: Image Books, 1964), p. 185.

page 121   "Do not, I beg you, address God": Ibid., p. 161.

page 122   Experiences, however moving, that leave us with a sense:
                  Ruth Burrows, *Guidelines to Mystical Prayer* (London: Sheed
                  & Ward, 1976), pp. 34, 52-55.

page 122   "When you speak, as it is right for you to do": Teresa of
                  Ávila, *The Way of Perfection*, p. 156.

page 123   "I am not asking you now to think of Him": Ibid., p. 174.

page 124   "the eyes of your soul": Ibid.

page 124   "A fine humility it would be": Ibid., p. 184.

page 125   "ask Him for things as we should": Ibid.

page 125   "See, He is only waiting for us to look at Him": Ibid., p. 174.

page 126   "If Thou, Lord, art willing to suffer": Ibid., pp. 175-76.

page 127   "O sisters, those of you whose minds cannot reason": Ibid.,
                  p. 173.

page 127   "shut themselves up in this way": Ibid., p. 185.

page 128   "make the slight effort necessary for recollection": Ibid., pp.
                  176-77.

page 128   To this he adds the conviction that God is always: Brother
                  Lawrence, *The Practice of the Presence of God*, p. 23.

pages 128-29   "I shall never do otherwise if You leave me": Ibid., pp. 29, 31.

page 129   "You have outwitted me": Ibid., p. 24.

page 129   "My God, I cannot do this unless You enable me": Ibid., p. 29.

page 129   "an habitual, silent and secret conversation": Ibid., p. 55.

page 129   "take delight in and become accustomed to His divine com-
                  pany": Ibid., p. 87.

pages 129-30   "we should stop as often as we can, for a moment": Ibid.,
                  p. 88.

page 130   "with greater happiness and satisfaction than that of an in-
                  fant nursing": Ibid., p. 56.

page 130   "Sometimes I think of myself as a block of stone": Ibid.

page 131   "Present yourself in prayer to God like a dumb": Ibid., pp. 63-64.

page 132   "I think, if I had understood then, as I do now": Teresa of Ávila, *The Way of Perfection*, p. 188.

page 133   "Faith becomes more alive and more active in every occasion": Brother Lawrence, *The Practice of the Presence of God*, p. 99.

page 133   "any such words that love may beget on the spur of the moment": Ibid., p. 98.

page 134   "One can at least . . . acquire by the practice": Ibid., p. 100.

Chapter 7: Praying with the Puritans: Meditation in Writing

page 136   "For me writing has always felt like praying": Marilyn Robinson, *Gilead* (New York: Farrar, Strauss and Giroux, 2004), p. 19.

page 138   However, if you read what actual Puritans wrote: Charles Hambrick-Stowe has made the case convincingly that the Puritans are best defined by these spiritual disciplines that shaped the way they understood the Christian life. See his books *The Practice of Piety: Puritan Devotional Disciplines in Seventeenth-Century New England* (Chapel Hill: University of North Carolina Press, 1982) and *Early New England Meditative Poetry: Anne Bradstreet and Edward Taylor* (New York: Paulist, 1988).

page 139   Samuel set up a stone as a reminder : John Beadle, *The Journal or Diary of a Thankful Christian* (London: E. Cotes, 1656). The Samuel text is pictured as the frontispiece, and the Numbers text is the motto on the title page.

page 139   Providence filled Beadle with a sense of wonder: Ibid., pp. 66-67.

page 139   "The rest sit round it, and pluck blackberries": Elizabeth Barrett Browning, "Aurora Leigh," seventh book.

page 139   "1. Let every man keep a strict account": Beadle, *Journal*, p. 48.

page 140   "2. Take speciall notice of all divine assistance": Ibid., p. 51.

page 141   "3. Remember, and for that end put into your Journal": Ibid., p. 55.

page 141   "4. All the instruments, all the men and means": Ibid., p. 58.

page 141   "5. And finally, mark what returns": Ibid., p. 62.

page 142   "For want of this examination": Thomas Hooker, "The Character of a Sound Christian in Seventeen Markes," in *The Paterne of Perfection* (London: Printed by R. Young, 1640), pp. 376-92. This quotation is from p. 390.

page 143   "If when thou mournest": Ibid., p. 378.

page 143   "If thou canst chide thy owne heart": Ibid., p. 380.

page 144   "If thou canst be patient under afflictions": Ibid., p. 381.

page 144   "If thou art as well content": Ibid., p. 383.

page 145   "Let the first part be, to *Inform* our selves": [Cotton Mather], *Christianus per Ignem; Or, a Disciple WARMING of himself and OWNING of his Lord: With Devout and Useful MEDITATIONS, Fetch'd out of the FIRE, By a Christian in a Cold Season, Sitting Before It* (Boston: B. Green and J. Allen, 1702), pp. 9-10. All capitalization and italics in the quotations are as in the original.

page 145   "All the *Creatures* of God about us": Ibid., pp. 10-11, 12.

page 146   "I am going to Discourse *with* and *on* my fire": Ibid., pp. 47-48. For the boast that prompted the book, see p. 15.

page 146   He summarizes the method as a triangular journey: Ibid., pp. 13-14. Mather cites Hugh of St. Victor (c. 1096-1141) for the second step, the *"three fold Voice* of all the Creatures unto us *Accipe, Redde, Fugue."*

page 146   As a fire can be smothered if the wood is piled too closely: Mather, *Christianus per Ignem*, pp. 140, 143-50, 60-63, 165-66, 159, 170.

page 148   "But when shall I be capable of proclaiming": Saint Augustine *Confessions* 11.2(2), trans. Henry Chadwick (Oxford: Oxford University Press, 1991), p. 221.

page 148   "Grant me chastity and continence": *Confessions* 7.7(17), p. 145.

page 148   "With your word you pierced my heart": *Confessions* 10.6(8), p. 183.

page 149   "It altered my prayers": *Confessions* 3.4(7), p. 39.

page 149   At the same time, God even used Augustine's sins: *Confessions* 5.8(14-15), pp. 80-81.

page 149   "in your deep counsel you heard the central point": *Confessions* 5.8(15)-9(16), pp. 82-83.

page 150   He calls himself "a vast problem": *Confessions* 4.4(9), p. 57, and 10.17(26), p. 194.

page 150   "When I did not get my way": *Confessions* 1.6(8), p. 7.

page 150   "These inferior goods have their delights": *Confessions* 2.5(9-10), pp. 29-30.

page 151   "We cease to find our joy in your truth": *Confessions*
                  10.36(59), p. 214.

Chapter 8: Praying with *The Cloud of Unknowing*:
Contemplation in the Dark

page 155   the mystical element of Christianity offered by Bernard Mc-
                  Ginn: Bernard McGinn, *The Foundations of Mysticism: Ori-*
                  gins to the Fifth Century, The Presence of God, vol. 1 (New
                  York: Crossroad, 1991), p. xvii.

page 157   at one point the author of the *Cloud* says: *The Cloud of Un-*
                  knowing, ed. James Walsh, Classics of Western Spirituality
                  (New York: Paulist, 1981), chap. 70, p. 256.

page 160   perhaps the best starting place is to read *The Life of Moses*:
                  Gregory of Nyssa, *The Life of Moses,* trans. Everett Ferguson
                  and Abraham J. Malherbe, Classics of Western Spirituality
                  (Mahwah, N.J.: Paulist, 1978).

page 161   You have to get familiar enough with it: See *Cloud of Un-*
                  knowing, chap. 4, pp. 121-22, 124.

page 162   "But no man can think of God himself": Ibid., chap. 6, pp.
                  130-31.

page 162   "With a devout, pleasing": Ibid., chap. 6, p. 131.

page 162   "For in the spiritual realm, height and depth": Ibid., chap.
                  37, p. 193.

page 162   People who do that just get exhausted: See ibid., chap. 57, pp.
                  230-31, and chap. 60, pp. 238-39.

page 164   If you are trying to gaze up toward God: See ibid., chap. 5,
                  p. 129.

page 165   Tell them you know they are there: See ibid., chap. 7, pp.
                  131-33.

page 165   "Cower down under them like a poor wretch": Ibid., chap.
                  32, p. 181. See also chaps. 31-32, pp. 179-83.

page 166   Slow and gentle repetition of an appropriate word: See ibid.,
                  chap. 7, pp. 133-34; chaps. 36-40, pp. 190-98.

page 168   No matter what you experience, there is a cloud: See ibid.,
                  chaps. 71-72, pp. 257-60.

Chapter 9: Praying with Agnes Sanford: *The Healing Light*

page 180   "Heavenly Father, please increase in me": Agnes Sanford,
                  The Healing Light, 2nd ed. (St. Paul, Minn.: Macalester Park
                  Publishing, 1947), p. 22. All quotations are from this edi-

tion. Later versions were revised at many points.

page 180   "We find after a while that we desire God more": Ibid., p. 71.

page 180   "we must decide on some tangible thing": Ibid., p. 22.

page 183   Her adviser told her to be with the sick boy: Ibid., p. 27; compare p. 39.

page 183   "Christ is the healer": Ibid., p. 115.

page 183   "The essence of all healing is to become so immersed": Ibid., p. 116.

page 184   She is convinced that "joy is the heavenly 'O.K.'": Ibid., p. 18.

page 184   "When our belief is weak": Ibid., p. 40.

page 184   "If we try this as a solemn duty": Ibid., pp. 29, 68.

page 185   Then we can ask Jesus to come: Ibid., pp. 145-47.

page 185   "harnessing the imagination and training the will": Ibid., p. 28.

page 186   "No matter what you want to make": Ibid., p. 35.

page 186   "When we ask for the indwelling of God's Holy Spirit": Ibid., p. 28.

page 187   "I give thanks that the shining of the Holy Spirit": Ibid., p. 41.

page 187   "See the bone all built in and the flesh strong": Ibid., p. 35.

page 188   "Pretend you're a big guy going to High School": Ibid., p. 29.

page 190   one will do better with MacNutt: Francis MacNutt, Healing (Notre Dame, Ind.: Ave Maria Press, 1974).

page 191   "One plain fact I dare to state": Sanford, Healing Light, p. 82.

page 191   "in certain very difficult cases there are adjustments": Ibid., p. 25.

page 191   "Someday we will understand the scientific principles": Ibid., pp. 19-20.

page 191   "the same principle is true of the creative energy": Ibid., p. 17.

Chapter 10: Praying with Andrew Murray: The Ministry of Intercession

page 195   "Let us beware of weakening the Word": Andrew Murray, With Christ in the School of Prayer: Thoughts on Our Training for the Ministry of Intercession (London: James Nisbet & Co., 1887), p. 34.

page 195   the earliest person I have found to use the term "prayer warriors": Andrew Murray, Aids to Devotion: Thoughts on the Holy Spirit in the Epistle to the Ephesians (London: James Nisbet & Co., 1909), p. 108.

page 197   "where there is true faith": Murray, With Christ in the School of Prayer, p. 78.

page 197	"The best way of learning to do a thing": Andrew Murray, *The Ministry of Intercession: A Plea for More Prayer* (New York: Revell, 1898), p. 192.
page 197	"Begin by setting apart some time every day": Ibid., pp. 192-93.
pages 197-98	"Just like the Lord, each believing intercessor has his own": Murray, *With Christ in the School of Prayer*, p. 217.
page 198	"While, on the one hand, the heart must be enlarged": Murray, *Ministry of Intercession*, p. 194.
page 198	"It is not with this will of God": Murray, *With Christ in the School of Prayer*, pp. 232-33.
page 198	"for kings and all rulers; for all who are in adversity": Murray, *Ministry of Intercession*, p. 193.
page 199	"It is of extreme importance that we should prove": Ibid., p. 194.
page 199	"In quiet, persistent, and determined perseverance": Murray, *With Christ in the School of Prayer*, p. 122.
page 199	while God's delay in answering exercises patience: Ibid., p. 121.
page 199	"What our prayer avails depends upon what we are": Ibid., pp. 201-2.
page 200	"it will not be difficult to say what is needed": Ibid., p. 249.
page 200	"In all God's intercourse with us": Ibid., p. 160.
page 200	"the glory of the Father must be the aim": Ibid., p. 152.
page 201	"No one would give another the free use of his name": Ibid., p. 187.
page 201	"Lord Jesus! Let Thy Spirit dwell in me, and fill me": Ibid., p. 193.
page 201	"It is as our faith grows into obedience": Ibid., p. 164; see pp. 160-69.
page 202	"That is, let thine eye be open to the Living God": Ibid., pp. 87-88.
page 202	"Just place yourself before, and look up into": Ibid., p. 19.
page 202	"It is Thyself living in me as in the Father": Ibid., p. 167.
page 203	"God needs, greatly needs, priests": Ibid., p. 245.
page 203	"Seek now to walk before the Lord in the full consciousness": Ibid., p. 246.

The Kneeling with Giants Reader:
Writings on Prayer by History's Best Teachers
Edited by Gary Neal Hansen

A COMPLIMENTARY COMPANION VOLUME INCLUDED
IN THE E-BOOK EDITION OF *KNEELING WITH GIANTS*.

If you want to know more about the ways of prayer in this book, then the *Kneeling with Giants Reader* will take you to the writings of the Giants themselves. Though designed for use in classes and study groups, it will also interest those who want to explore further on their own.

The *Reader* has a full chapter of primary source material corresponding to each of the ten chapters of *Kneeling with Giants,* with selections chosen to clearly introduce each approach to prayer in its original context.

- The best modern translations of non-English works

- Hard to find works, including three Puritan texts

- Four complete "hours" of the pre-Vatican II Benedictine daily office so that readers can experience the cycle of Benedictine prayer with ease

Find the e-book edition of *Kneeling with Giants,* including the *Kneeling with Giants Reader,* at your favorite ebook resellers, including Amazon, Barnes & Noble, Christian Book Distributors, Google, Kobo, eChristian and many more.

About the Author

You can connect with the author at GaryNealHansen.com.

Join his free member library for *Kneeling with Giants* small group resources:

- A free PDF Small Group Leader's Guide
- A discount offer for small groups or adult classes to purchase copies of *Kneeling with Giants*
- A free introductory video to jump-start your group's time with the book
- An invitation for your small group to have Gary join you via Skype

Find the member library at https://garynealhansen.com/library.

Sign up for the author's newsletter to read more from his current projects and hear about upcoming classes and other projects: http://bit.ly/GaryNealHansenNewsletter.